TEA GARDENING
FOR BEGINNERS

A Complete Beginner's Guide to Learn to Grow and Brew Your Own Tea at Home

JIMSON LEWIS

Table of Contents

Introduction

Tea gardening has a rich history and cultural background. According to historical evidence, tea drinking became a daily habit in the 3rd century CE. However, the plants used were grown for medicinal purposes long before that. Tea cultivation has laid the foundation for modern medicine. Yet, the traditional methods of preparing healing drinks from these plants haven't been lost either. As you'll learn from this guidebook, growing tea is one of the easiest ways to learn the basics of gardening.

Before you begin planting your garden, you'll need to familiarize yourself with the basics of tea farming. This book will list all the tools you need for planting, growing, harvesting, and preparing tea. You'll learn that teas require specific growing conditions, including soil and agro-climatic conditions. Depending on the amount of space you have, you'll need to decide where to establish your garden. This will also affect which species and varieties you'll be able to grow.

There is a wide range of tea species you can grow at home. There are chapters dedicated to giving you a list of recommended teas, as well as plenty of practical instructions on how to plant them, and for beginners, we've listed a number of easy-to-grow herbs and their purposes. You'll also learn how to identify diseased plants and what to do about them. Once your herbs have matured, you can refer to the harvesting instructions for safe, long-term preservation.

Learning adequate planting and harvesting methods is crucial for successful tea farming, and together with understanding proper storage conditions, it will help you get the most out of your tea garden. You'll have a pantry full of different herbs, which will come in handy for creating homemade tea blends. The book will help you master this unique art and take your tea-making skills to the next level.

You'll be introduced to the most common tea brewing methods. As you'll learn from the chapter listing these, the way you brew your tea has an enormous impact on the flavor and medicinal benefits of the herbs. Not only that, but the book will also explain the benefits of choosing the appropriate brewing method for each plant part.

Last but not least, you'll be introduced to two of the most popular uses for teas, creating blends for anxiety and headaches. In these modern times, many people are dealing with these issues, and the solution offered by Western medicine can sometimes do more harm than good. On the other hand, certain blends of teas have a natural way of soothing the nervous system, which is often enough to relieve anxiety and pain. If you're ready to explore these and other benefits of using teas you've cultivated on your own tea farm, continue reading.

Chapter 1

Basics of Tea Gardening

Tea farming is one of the oldest forms of plant cultivation in history. This chapter will introduce you to the origins of tea gardening. It delves into the historical and cultural background of tea brewing and cultivation, illustrating how this art has evolved over time. You'll learn how tea farming has shaped medicine, both in the traditional and modern sense. You'll also be given a list of equipment you'll need and a list of the best types of tea plants for creating a successful garden.

The History of Tea

The earliest tangible records indicate that tea cultivation began in the middle of the 3rd century CE in China. Some archeological records suggest that a couple of thousand years before, tea cultivation was also happening in Mesopotamia. However, this information is only based on the rich history of herbal use by the ancient Mesopotamians. According to Chinese lore, tea was discovered by Emperor Shen Nung. He was boiling water, and the wind blew leaves from the tea plant into the water. The emperor noticed that brew had a pleasant aroma and decided to try it. He observed the liquid warming up his body and wanted to learn more about making brews like this. After naming the liquid "ch'a" (which means "to check" in Chinese), he introduced it to others. The "ch'a" is a written character traditionally illustrated with grass, wooden branches, and a figure of a man standing between the two. For the Chinese, this character symbolizes the balance tea creates between nature and the people drinking it.

Initially, the brew was only used medicinally, but this changed rapidly. Soon everyone was drinking it for pleasure. As its popularity grew and it became a daily habit, tea plantation owners and merchants were soon making a fortune. Although, at that time, only green tea was grown, new and more exclusive blends were created and sold to the wealthy members of the Empire. It was believed that these were also specific because they were tended by young women, who were pure and couldn't taint the medicinal effect of the herbs. These young maidens were forbidden to handle or even eat spices to avoid contaminating the tea leaves.

The Chinese only discovered the process of making black tea in the middle of the 17th century, when the increase in foreign trade prompted them to investigate different preservation procedures. This was when the oxidation and fermentation processes were developed, and tea leaves with zestier flavors were produced. This new black tea kept its aroma for longer, which made it excellent for export and shipping. Since then, even more, tea-making methods have been discovered, and tea has remained an integral part of Chinese culture until this day.

The first territory tea was introduced to outside of China was the Tibetan Empire. Since the rough terrain and harsh climate made it impossible to cultivate this plant in Tibet, the Tibetans started to import tea from China at the beginning of the 9th century. Soon tea took over Tibet as well, even becoming more popular than it was in China. Not only were the dry leaves considered a staple in Tibetan culture, but they were used as currency over an extended period. Wealthy members of the society often paid servants and other laborers with tea, much to the lower ranks' happiness. Traditionally, tea in Tibet is made by boiling loose leaves for 30 minutes before straining and enriching them with salt and yak butter. This was a way those living at high altitudes replaced the salt and fat they'd lost during the day. To this day, Tibetans drink up to 40 cups of tea per day per person.

Around the 9th century, tea was introduced to Japan by a Buddhist monk named Dengyo Daishi, who brought tea seeds home after returning from his studies in China. In Japan, tea was first only consumed in monasteries as it was believed to have a spiritually enlightening effect. In fact, monks used tea as an energizing brew, which allowed them to stay focused during prolonged meditation exercises. By the beginning of the 14th century, the art of tea brewing had become popular in Japanese society, albeit it was still largely associated with spiritual practices. The sacred Japanese tea ceremony was developed in the 15th century. This is a way of celebrating the art of brewing and drinking tea. It was developed by Zen Buddhists, who used this act to honor the Japanese spiritual philosophy. The ceremony has become so popular that, in many houses, additional rooms were built for brewing tea. Women who wished to marry were required to master the art of the traditional tea ceremony. The Japanese used Matcha tea (a form of green tea). They combine it with a small amount of water, which results in a potent, earthy flavor. Later, fermented and steeped teas also became popular - although these teas have a much stronger flavor than traditional green tea. The Japanese also revolutionized tea production by switching to specialized machines as soon as technology made this possible.

During the rise of the 17th-century trade period, tea also made its way to Russia and Europe. Tea was transported to Russia by a camel caravan (a journey that took over a year to make between China and Russia) until the beginning of the 20th century, which marked the opening of the Trans-Siberian Railway. Tea was introduced to Europe by Dutch and Portuguese merchants. It was first known as a brew with spiritually lifting, invigorating, and medicinal properties. Later, when a Portuguese princess married King Charles II of England, tea drinking became a status symbol across Europe. Since it was still considered a novelty, import prices of tea were high, and only the wealthiest members of society could afford it. The ability to drink tea appropriately was taught to the aristocratic young people, and wealthy families were often painted drinking tea.

The elitist British society created several traditions involving teas. One of these is the "Afternoon Tea," a novelty custom created to fill the gap between breakfast and the evening meal. Until then, the aristocracy only had two main meals a day - the first being a light repast, while the second was served very late. The "Afternoon tea" was served alongside a light meal and soon became popular. "High tea" is Another British tea-drinking tradition. Despite its elite-sounding name, it was invented by the working class in the 19th century. It had a similar purpose to "Afternoon tea." However, this one is served with a full meal, which fulfills working people's needs for a substantial meal that provides plenty of energy.

When the Chinese placed an embargo on tea exports to Britain, the British resorted to growing their own. A Scottish botanist named Robert Fortune learned the traditional Chinese tea processing techniques while studying plants in China. Fortune started cultivating tea plants in the place he considered to have the best climate for this, India. The country had its own indigenous tea plants, and by the mid-19th century, it was invaded by the British. Fortune took a small group of Chinese tea growers to India who taught local farmers all the tea farming secrets. Soon after, India (and, by extension, Britain) was able to cultivate the best quality tea plants.

As the Europeans colonized the New World, North America became the newest tea-brewing continent. It first appeared as part of the European etiquette brought over by wealthy families from the mainland. However, tea soon became one of the most imported products in North America, which the British tried to profit from by raising export taxes. This was followed by the American War of Independence, after which tea consumption in North America changed drastically. It stopped being an elitist tradition, and the Americans had put their own spin on tea brewing. They invented iced tea, which was created as a refreshing drink for hot summer days in the early 20th century. An American merchant is credited with the invention of tea bags. After shipping their product to restaurants in silk bags, the merchant discovered that the establishments didn't remove the loose leaves from the small satchels but brewed them in the bags. Soon, they started to market tea sold in small bags as a more efficient tea brewing solution.

Nowadays, people are re-discovering the traditional benefits of teas across all continents. Those wanting to substitute unhealthy beverages, like calorie-filled soft drinks and modern coffees, often turn to teas. Besides the traditional tea plant, the name has been given to many beverages now made from different herbs, spices, and plants. All these have their specific uses and health benefits. There are also long-standing folk traditions of making infusions, decoctions, and other tea-like remedies. These were present in many cultures and developed independently from the Chinese tea cultivating and brewing tradition. As people discovered the benefits of teas, they linked this knowledge to folk medicine traditions.

More and more plants were added to the list of teas people could grow, harvest, and prepare in their homes, making tea more accessible to everyone.

Teas (as well as infusions and decoctions) have even shaped Western medicine. Namely, many modern artificial drugs were created to mimic the effects of traditional teas, infusions, and decoctions. At first, these contained the same herbs the teas were made of. However, after the industrial revolutions popularized mass production, it became more profitable to use artificial ingredients that mimic medicinal herbs. However, since this type of medicine has many more side effects, drinking medicinal teas is an infinitely healthier option. Hence the growth in popularity of natural teas and tea cultivation has been seen in the past years. Although herbal teas can't replace Western medicine, they have plenty of health benefits. If you're only looking to add a healthy brew into your life, growing your own teas is the best possible way to do so. Tea farming doesn't have to take much space, time, or money, yet it allows you to stock plenty of healthy blends in your pantry.

The Basic Tools of Tea Gardening

Now that you've learned how people discovered the benefits of the different teas, it's time to look into the tools required for tea gardening. For planting the herbs, you'll need the following:

- **Flowers, herbs, and other types of plants for tea** - Before choosing anything else, you should consider which type of plants you want to grow. This will help determine factors like growing conditions and supplies. Depending on your space, time, climate, and the plants you've chosen, you can propagate from seeds, seedlings, or plant parts (leaves, roots, etc.)

- **Pots and containers** - You can use pots of various sizes and shapes, depending on the amount of space you have available and where you plan to establish your garden. Buying plastic containers in bulk is the most economical solution. Make sure they have an efficient draining system and also are not made from any toxic material that could affect the propagation of your plants.

- **Raised beds** - If you're cultivating tea in your yard, you'll also need adequate plant beds. Raised beds have an excellent draining system, which is essential for healthy plant development. They allow the plants to absorb just the right amount of water and nutrition and make gardening much easier.

- **Garden soil** - Whether you plant in indoor pots or your yard, topsoil is essential for gardening. You'll learn more about the importance of choosing the appropriate growth medium in the next chapter.

- **Hand trowel** - It will come in handy for making holes for seeds and plants and later for maintenance. It should have a narrow blade and a comfortable grip.

- **Shovels, spades, forks, hoes, and rakes** - These are used for moving the soil, digging, and distributing natural fertilizer. They'll also be needed for removing weeds. You'll only need them if you're planting in your garden.

- **Garden hose or watering can** - You'll need a water hose for soaking the ground before planting herbs in the garden. If you're planting in pots, you'll use a watering can instead.

- **Gardening gloves** - Having a few pairs of gardening gloves is a must, regardless of the size of your garden. Look for gloves made of good quality material that'll provide adequate protection from staining, drying out, and sharp plant parts.

- **Padded kneelers** - If you're creating a large garden, you'll be on your knees a lot during your work. With adequate kneelers, you can protect your knees from straining and injuries. They also protect your clothes, just as gloves protect your hands.

- **Planners** - This is an optional tool, but it can be extremely useful when planting several different herbs. You can note down planting dates, propagation dates, growth rates, issues you encounter with certain plants, reminders, or anything else you want to create evidence of on your gardening journey.

- **Labels** - Another optional tool you can use to make gardening easier. Labeling the plants in your garden helps you to keep track of their development and avoid mistakes during harvesting.

Next are the supplies you'll need for maintaining your garden and harvesting:

- **Soil monitor** - This handy device will enable you to track pH, water, and climate condition. It makes it easier to know when to water the plants and whether they're getting enough nutrition and sun.

- **Pruners** - Essential tools for cutting and removing plants and plant parts. The most highly recommended option is the bypass-style pruner because it provides the quickest cut and causes less injury to the plants. If you've planted larger plants, you'll probably need a telescoping pruner to reach every branch.

- **Gardening knives and scissors** - These are also used for pruning, removing diseased plants, and thinning if needed for better propagation.

- **Watering wands** - Similar to cans, watering wands are used for watering plants in pots and smaller indoor or outdoor containers. Watering wands let you reach higher and ensure an adequate moisture level in overhead baskets and pots.

- **Rakes** - If you're planting in your garden, you'll need a tool for collecting weeds, herbs you'll use for teas, and leftover plant material you have no use for. Leaf rakes are the best option for this purpose.

- **Wheelbarrow** - Another piece of equipment you need for collecting plants from your garden (although it can come in handy during planting too). It makes carrying pots, plants, and supplies to and from your garden much easier.

- **Herb stripper** - This handy tool is perfect for stripping leaves when you're harvesting plants for loose-leaf teas. For practical reasons, getting one for stripping multiple sizes is recommended.

Different Types of Tea

When one thinks of tea, the first types that come to mind are black and green teas. Both of these are made from the plant called Camelia sinensis (also called Thea sinensis). Initially, only two varieties of this plant were used for making tea - the Assam plant (C. sinensis variety assamica) and the China plant (C. sinensis variety sinensis). Nowadays, over 3000 varieties of different plants are used for making this delicious beverage - and this is not counting the blends! Not only do the different varieties define the tea's flavor profile but also plant growing conditions. That said, here are the basic types of tea available:

- **Green tea**: Made from un-oxidized tea leaves, therefore able to retain their evergreen color. The leaves are either steamed, pan-fired, or dried through specific methods. It has a delicate flavor.

- **Yellow tea:** Processed like green tea without oxidation. However, the drying process is much slower, and the leaves have a naturally yellowish color. It's the rarest form of tea, with a flavor milder than green tea.

- **Black tea**: Made from fully oxidized tea leaves, a process that causes them to wither and get darker in color. It has a much stronger flavor than black tea.

- **Oolong tea:** Produced from partially oxidized tea leaves. The oxidation level determines the zest of the flavor, which can range from mild as green tea to almost as strong as black tea.

- **White tea**: Made from barely oxidized tea leaves. They're dried very slowly (similarly to the natural withering process), which gives them a soft flavor, much like green tea, except sweeter.

- **Pu-erh:** An earthly flavored tea created by slow fermentation of tea leaves. It's kept underground for years and sold compressed into round shapes.

- **Yerba mate:** Produced from a plant with a bittersweet flavor with an energizing effect. It's a naturally caffeinated herbal tea.

- **Guayusa:** Made from a plant with an earthy flavor and sweet aftertaste. Like the previous one, this one is also naturally caffeinated.

- **Herbal teas**: Any tea or infusion made from a plant other than Camelia sinensis varieties is called herbal tea. They can be made from almost any common herb with medicinal properties. You can use seeds, roots, berries, leaves, bark, flowers of herbs, spices, vegetables, fruits, and other plants.

Chapter 2

Growing Conditions

Where Do Tea Plants Grow?

There are actually three parts to this question: Do these plants like steep or flat terrain, what regions of the globe do they thrive in, and what sort of climate is best for growing tea plants?

Each tea has its own distinct flavor for several reasons, and these questions all have an influence on that profile. It's always a combination of factors, including how it's prepared, the soil it's grown in, and the plant species involved.

Because the questions are interconnected, let's start with the fundamentals of each.

What Is the Best Climate to Cultivate Tea Plants?

Tea plants are native to the tropics and subtropics. These are the places where they first evolved. Tea plants have been transplanted to far-flung locations with drastically different climates and geologies than their native home.

They are now cultivated in numerous places across the globe. Asia, Africa, and South America are the primary tea-growing areas, with the world's largest tea producers being China, Kenya, Sri Lanka, India, and Vietnam.

The quality of tea cultivated in any region is determined partly by the region's climate.

Tea plants thrive in tropical and subtropical regions, although they often need high humidity and considerable rainfall throughout the growing season. Many diverse climatic conditions, however, might be favorable for tea growth.

Some of the climatic conditions required for the cultivation of tea plants are explained below.

Tea Cultivation Temperature

Tea harvest time in any given year depends on the average temperature of that year.

Tea needs mild to warm temperatures and at least five to six hours of direct sunlight daily. Tea plants' ideal yearly temperature range is between 15 and 23 degrees Celsius. They need a total annual temperature of between 3,500 and 4,000 degrees Celsius.

An excess or a lack of temperature could affect or prevent tannins from forming in tea. The tannin buildup is interrupted when the temperature exceeds 35 degrees Celsius. However, tea leaves will burn if the temperature is above 35 degrees for an extended period.

Low, as opposed to high temperatures, cause changes in tea buds' physical and biochemical makeup, which will negatively affect the development of the tea plant and the buds' quality.

There are fewer active ingredients, caffeine, and catechins in tea cultivated at higher temperatures compared to tea grown at lower temperatures.

Tea Cultivation Rainfall

The duration of the growing season and the time until it's ready to harvest are both affected by the total amount and distribution of rainfall. This affects the size of the harvest.

If your plantation gets around 1,500 mm of rain annually, equally divided across the months, you can be pretty sure your harvest will be good. Minimum rainfall is at least 1,000 mm, with at least 50 mm falling each month. Watering has a noticeable productive impact in various tea-growing regions. Watering studies, like in Vietnam, indicated a 41.5% increase in bud output compared to their non-irrigated counterparts. The tea buds subjected to water improved considerably in quality.

Tea Cultivation Humidity

Young leaves and buds are plucked from a tea plant to make tea, and it needs a high level of moisture to thrive. Tea needs high air humidity; the ideal is about 85% throughout the growing season.

Buds and new leaves flourish in the damp, foggy, and dewy conditions of early morning. Humidity levels below 70% hurt tea growth and production.

Tea's development and flavor are profoundly impacted by the humidity of its environment. The tea plant develops well when there is enough dampness. There are huge, tender leaves, new buds, and an overall trend toward improved quality.

Bud development is stunted if there isn't enough water, humidity, or soil moisture. Low humidity level causes the leaves to thicken and harden, forming many buds of poor quality.

What Effect Can Climate Change Have on Tea Leaves?

Climate change usually affects the amount of tea that planters can cultivate. Although climate change impacts each location differently, it broadly impacts tea output by changing the amount of precipitation, raising temperatures, adjusting season timing, and boosting the population of insect pests.

The effects of climate change on rainfall causes it to swing between extreme drought and severe downpours.

The ground erodes and becomes soggy as a result of the heavy rains. It also harms root growth and affects tea plant output.

Because of climate change, tea harvests may be reduced, particularly for the first and second flushes. As temperatures increase, they also diminish the quality of the tea and have resulted in low yields.

Like most food crops, the temperature plays havoc with crop growth or lack thereof. The fluctuations affect dormant, non-reproductive buds, which will eventually reduce yield. Pests also become more of a problem in these temperature conditions, increasing the havoc they wreak on tea crops.

Choosing a region with ideal climatic conditions is essential for efficient, profitable tea growth, and the detrimental effects of climate change on tea farming must also be taken into account.

What Is the Best Soil Type to Cultivate Tea Plants?

Many soil types are used for growing tea, each with its geographical background. A soil with a pH between 4.5 and 5.5, a medium-to-high organic matter status, and adequate drainage is ideal for growing tea.

High-altitude, rich soil on the edge of a mountain range is perfect. Ideally, tea plants should be grown in loose, deep soil. There should be at least 1.5 m of soil depth between the topsoil and the bedrock.

Shallow soil inhibits root development. Add to that the threat of drought, and you are wasting your time by trying to cultivate tea in these conditions.

At What Height Above Sea Level Should Tea Plants Be Cultivated?

Almost all black tea traded internationally originates from highland locations. You will find the most professionally maintained tea plantations in the hills or slopes with adequate natural drainage of a tropical country. Tea cannot grow in standing water; therefore, waterlogged lowlands are unsuitable for growing tea.

Different elevations produce different quality teas; for example, "Low Crown Tea" is cultivated at a height of fewer than 610 meters, "Medium Crown Tea" is produced between 610 and 1,200 meters, and "High Crown Tea" is cultivated on lands at an altitude of 1,220 meters or above.

Nearly anywhere you find tea in the monsoon countries, you'll discover gardens built into the side of a mountain. The best land for growing tea is hilly and heavily forested, so water can drain away quickly, and the soil doesn't get washed out too much.

What Is the Ideal Distance between Plants?

Plantings in a commercial context might have a distance between 1.5 and 3 feet between each seedling. However, a minimum distance of five feet between your small home gardens should be left between each plant. For the best possible tea harvesting results, it is recommended that you do not prune your tea plants often.

Ideal Shade for Cultivating Tea Plants

Tea plants thrive better when protected from direct sunlight or strong winds. Plantations often practice interspersing shrubs with larger trees for the dual purpose of shading the tea plants and the workers who work on them.

Labor Requirements for Tea Plants

Preparing fields, weeding, trimming, and harvesting are all year-round tasks on tea farms. Tea planting and processing are time-consuming and labor-intensive processes. Tea plucking is laborious and requires expertise and patience.

All picking is done by hand, and workers are compensated based on the quantity of tea they harvest each day. There must be workers at the tea processing factories to dry, roll, ferment, sift, grade, and package the leaves.

Capital Requirements for Tea Plants

Tea growing on an industrial scale is a capital-intensive business. Tea planting requires enormous sums of money for plantation expansion, laborer pay, and processing.

Latitude Range for Growing Tea Plants

The ideal latitude range for growing tea is between 42 and 33 degrees north and south. However, 35° North in Japan and 8° South in Java, both firmly inside the tropical and subtropical zones, is where most of the world's commercial tea is grown.

In this region, the colder temperatures are better for the China bush, one of the two primary types of tea plants, while the warmer, more humid climates are ideal for the Assam bush.

Temperatures often drop farther away from the equator. Latitude affects not just the distance from the sun but also the length of days and the existence or absence of different seasons. All of these factors affect ideal tea cultivation conditions.

Nutrient Requirement for Tea Plants

Tea plantations rely heavily on chemical fertilizers, making nutrient control an absolute must. Therefore, fertilizer application is an essential part of growing tea. The amount of fertilizer used is determined by various parameters, including the production of the portion, the kind of pruning, and the fertility state of the soil.

For efficient management, it is essential to establish a well-thought-out fertilizer program and to purchase fertilizers as needed. Another consideration is applying fertilizer at the proper time and using the proper guidelines.

Time of Fertilizer Application

- Fertilizer must be administered before the start of the monsoon season.

- Fertilizer should be used in March or April when the early spring showers have dampened the soil.

- Moisture should be present in the soil to a depth of 40 cm.

- Apply fertilizer to weed-free, cleared ground.

- Apply fertilizers once the plants have grown in unpruned areas.

- You should fertilize your sprouted tea or trim your tea plants after they've sprouted a few leaves.

- Remember to avoid applying fertilizer on wet days.

Nutritional Evaluation

Periodic soil and foliar analyses need to be done to know how effective your fertilization techniques and nutrient levels are. By comparing the amount of fertilizer used in the past with the amount of oil and biomass produced, farmers may get a good idea of how their crops will react to future applications.

Since there is no universally accepted maximum leaf level for a given nutrient, comparing the levels in a healthy and unwell plant might help pinpoint the source of a nutritional deficiency. A plant's yield largely depends on the soil's quality and the availability of nutrients.

Artificial fertilizers have enhanced agricultural output, including nitrogen, phosphorous, and potassium. Therefore, measures for improving agricultural productivity in impoverished nations should include nitrogen and phosphorus replenishment through microbial activities. It is possible to do this by using organic fertilizers. Nutritional analysis may be beneficial to:

- Determine inadequacies and toxicity.

- Create a fertilizer program.

- Determine the number of nutrients lost.

- Examine the nutritional status of the tea plantation.

- Compare the nutritional status of different areas.

Liquid Fertilizer

Regular fertilizer application helps the tea plant. Apply a consistent 10-10-10 liquid fertilizer to the plant every month while it's actively growing. For every 10 square feet, use one gallon of water and one-third of an ounce of liquid fertilizer.

Spread the fertilizer out throughout the soil using a broadcast sprayer. When spraying, move the sprayer back and forth.

Choosing the Right Plant to Cultivate According to Growing Conditions

Remarkably, 200 Camellia Theaceae species are recognized, with only Camellia sinensis utilized to make tea. There are several variants of this species:

1. Camellia Sinensis VAR. Sinensis

Sinesis is a Latin word for "from China," where tea was originally found. This type is claimed to be the oldest variety utilized in tea farming. It has tiny, black leaves with a light body. It has a potential height of 20 feet in its native environment.

Because it is a hardy plant that can withstand harsher circumstances, like those found in certain areas of China, Japan, Iran, and Turkey, it is often cultivated at higher elevations. It can live for over a century given the right circumstances, and its usefulness is guaranteed for at least that long.

2. Camellia Sinensis VAR Assamica

Major Robert Bruce of Scotland found this cultivar in the Indian state of Assam during the early part of the nineteenth century. This is widely cultivated in India, Africa, and Sri Lanka.

It is grown mostly on plains and in areas with adequate rainfall since it is well-suited to a tropical environment.

Its huge, thick leaves create a powerful black liquor when oxidized, although it is less fragrant than Camellia sinensis var. Sinensis leaves.

This is the tallest Camellia sinensis variety. In their natural habitat, these trees have been known to reach a height of 30 meters and survive for hundreds of years. However, under planting conditions, it only lasts 30 to 60 years.

3. Camellia Sinensis VAR Cambodiensis

Camellia sinensis var. Cambodiensis leaves are large and flexible, reaching a length of 20 cm, because their sensory traits are not as valued as those of C. Sinensis var. Sinensis and C.s. var. Assamica, C.s. var. Cambodiensis is seldom utilized for tea growing. However, its high natural hybridization capability with the other two kinds is sometimes used to generate new cultivars.

4. Camellia Sasanqua

Other, less common Camellia cultivars are also used to produce tea. Camellia sasanqua is one of these plants. This variety produces rich, clove-flavored tea. It is also known as the Yuletide Camellia because its blossoms are brilliant reddish pink rather than the traditional delicate white of the Sinensis varieties.

Camellia sasanqua is more than simply a pleasant drink. It's also an exceptionally stunning blooming shrub!

5. Camellia Japonica

Camellia japonica produces a profusion of pink flowers and thrives in temperatures ranging from the United Kingdom to Alabama.

It is both an excellent green tea and a beautiful decorative bush. You may find this variety in numerous nurseries all across North America.

The Cultivar

The word "cultivar," which is an abbreviation of the phrase "cultivated variation," refers to a species of plant that was formed by crossing or mutation and then chosen for its unique traits.

Because these qualities are not always transferred via sowing, the cultivars must be replicated by cuttings to maintain a similar genetic makeup.

Cross-breeding has been used extensively in the tea industry to create hybrids with improved climate and disease resistance and new and interesting flavors and scents.

Other Care Requirements for Your Tea Garden

1. Watering

Tea loves water, and your soil should always be damp. You should water your tea garden every day or two throughout the growing season (spring and summer). If your garden soil is too try, you could be infected by a spider mite, which can affect flowering.

Water the soil twice a month throughout the winter to keep it from drying. Early morning and late at night are the optimum times to water throughout the spring and summer. Midday is a bad time to water because of the high temperature and the rapid evaporation that will occur.

During the winter months, water your tea garden during the day instead of in the morning or evening, when the temperature is often too low and might cause damage to the roots. Watering with rainfall or distilled water is preferable. Do not use tap water for your tea garden because it is alkaline. To maintain consistent temperatures and humidity and to prevent weed development, a layer of bark eight centimeters thick may be applied to the soil's surface.

2. Pruning

Due to its moderate growth rate, don't prune your tea plants too much. Make sure you prune any dead, diseased, or low-growing branches, flowerless ones. Cutting off wilting flowers as soon as possible may minimize nutrient consumption, allowing the plant to grow more strongly and create new flower buds.

Tea Plant Container Requirements

When growing tea in a container, ensure the pot is at least twice as large as the root ball and has lots of drainage holes. You should use acidic potting soil and fill one-third of the container. Spread the soil out, then set the tea plant on top, leaving some space between the soil and the plant's crown.

Put the tea plant in a spot with a temperature of around 70 degrees Fahrenheit and brilliant, indirect sunlight. Water the plant regularly, but don't let the roots get saturated. Water until the drainage holes are completely dry.

Keep the container from sitting in water and give the soil time to drain. Let the top several inches (or 5–10 cm) of soil in between watering dry out. Tea plants you grow in containers need fertilizer from spring through fall when they are actively growing. Fertilize your plants every three weeks using an acidic fertilizer, diluted to half strength as directed by the manufacturer.

Prune your tea plants after they bloom each year. Take down any shaky or damaged branches as well. Reduce the shrub's height by about half if you want to control its size or encourage new growth. If the plant's roots start to grow too big for the container, you may either transplant it to a larger pot or prune the roots so they are more manageable. Repot as required, approximately every 2–4 years.

Essential Elements Needed for Tea Plant Growth

There are many nutrients needed for the adequate growth of tea plants. Some of these nutrients are explained below.

1. Nitrogen

Used to produce protoplasm and chlorophyll. Large amounts are necessary, and the dosage should be similar to that of potassium applications. Since nitrogen is so active in plants, a deficit will initially appear in the older leaves before spreading to the newer ones.

2. Phosphorus

It encourages vigorous root development. Many crops benefit from using phosphate fertilizers, like superphosphate, during their early stages of growth.

3. Potassium

Potassium is a component of photosynthesis and is vital for tea plants. It is often inadequate in locations with significant rain, sandy soils, and heavy harvesting of plants.

4. Copper

It aids in the production of chloroplasts and proteins. It is poor in sandy loam soils with a high pH. When deficient, it causes distorted and stunted development.

Foliar spray is used to apply copper sulfate or copper chelate. The amount needed for tea is quite small, and a decrease in its influence on agricultural output has only been seen on rare occasions.

5. Sulfur

Sulfur is required for photosynthesis since it forms proteins and chlorophyll. Sulfur gets depleted in waterlogged soils because it often dries out along with iron and manganese. Sulfur insufficiency is widely known in several tea-growing regions. The sulfur concentration in tea twigs ranges from 0.08 to 0.30% depending on dry matter, restricting tea output.

The yellowing of the leaf blades and the presence of deep veins down to the greatest branching point below characterize this deficit, called "Tea Yellows" in tiny leaves. Following that, they become green. The tea plant only requires 20 percent sulfur annually, which may be supplied using ammonium sulfate.

6. Magnesium and Calcium

Soil pH may be corrected by applying dolomite lime twice every cycle, taking care of calcium and magnesium nutrition. However, since magnesium and potassium are antagonistic, areas with greater potassium decrease magnesium availability. Tea farmers are advised to apply 1.0% magnesium sulfate to combat this negative relationship.

The required 7–9 kg of magnesium sulfate can be efficiently delivered through four to six foliar spray treatments. Since $Mg2+$ is a freely moving ion in the plant, its depletion usually shows up first in the oldest leaves. A magnesium shortage in tea plants often manifests as chlorosis in the veins, premature leaf drop, and yellowing of older leaves.

7. Manganese

Manganese is required to form the sugar and the action of enzymes. It is needed for plants to absorb phosphate and potassium. Its deficit is uncommon and occurs exclusively at high pH levels. Deficiency starts with the young leaves shrinking first. Manganese sulfate is used to cure deficiencies. Tea has a high manganese absorption rate and can withstand high element concentrations. The use of phosphate may increase manganese content.

When tea plants lack one or more micronutrients (Fe, Zn, Cu, etc.), they need much higher concentrations of other micronutrients (N, K, etc.). After harvest, rapid growth and the resulting reduction in the root system from trimming indicate a nutritional shortage. After a month or two of inactivity, the plants will have trouble getting enough nutrients to survive. Foliar nutrient application is beneficial in these situations.

You can't just start enjoying tea and consider yourself a tea connoisseur. The process begins with centuries-old customs and techniques that hone the taste of each leaf and enhance its visual appeal. The experience focuses on understanding how tea leaves are cultivated and collected and the conditions necessary for the laborious operation.

Tea is distinct not just because of the plant from which it is made but also how it's grown. With only a little tweaking of the ideal conditions, the same leaves may be transformed into a wide range of delicious and distinctive flavors. The next time you make a pot of tea, you should savor every sip and think about how much work went into making it.

Chapter 3

Deciding Where
to Grow Your Garden

The location of your garden is a vital consideration. Before you decide where to plant, look at what is available in your environment – what natural resources does your area have?

How much water is available, how hot or cold it gets, what kinds of nutrients, fertilizers, and other chemicals are readily available, and how much sun the garden receives all play a role in how well it grows. Your garden should receive at least five hours of sunlight per day, and the soil should be loose enough to drain water while also being very fertile.

Having your garden near other shrubs and trees could deplete the soil nutrients, so bear this in mind when making your decision.

When deciding where to grow your garden, consider the following factors carefully.

Factors to Consider When Choosing a Location for Your Garden

1. Availability of Sunlight

Your garden requires at least six to eight hours of sunlight per day to be productive throughout the year because photosynthesis, the only way plants produce energy, requires sunlight. So, if you t place your garden in an area where it won't get enough sunlight, there will be less photosynthesis, leading to less production. Before planting a garden, use one of these methods to determine how much sunlight will reach the soil.

Sun Charting: By making a chart of the sun, you can see how much light gets into different parts of your home. This will help you decide where to put your garden and which plants to cultivate for the best harvest.

Make a sun chart showing your intended garden location and add the hours between sunrise and sunset to the chart.

Check the proposed site every hour to see if it is fully or partially shaded. Do this for a few days to ensure you have reliable data.

After a week or less of observation, compile your data and compare the amount of sunlight in each area per day, the amount of shade, and the duration of both the sunlight and the shade. This will help you to build your garden in the right place in your home.

Creating a Map of the Shade: Make a site plan for your compound and make copies of it at 10 a.m., 1 p.m., and 4 p.m. Each copy should be labeled with the time it represents.

Visit the site at the specified time and color the areas with a shade at each time. Examine the three maps to determine where you have full sun, half sun, and shade.

Using Automated Tools: You can measure the sun's intensity using automated tools. You can place these tools in strategic locations throughout your compound each morning and leave them there for the entire day, then check the results the next morning. Reduce this process for 3 to 5 days to ensure the sun's consistency.

2. Soil Health

The health of your soil determines the health of your garden plants. The following parameters, which we will go over in detail, can be used to assess soil health: Fertility, looseness, and drainage capacity of the soil.

Soil Fertility: Loamy soils are the most fertile of all soil types and are ideal for gardening. Consider creating your garden in an area with this type of soil. When wet, loamy soil can be rolled into balls that are crumbly. This soil should be rich in organic materials and dark in color. A soil that is orange in color indicates a lack of organic materials in the ground. In this case, you should add leaf mulch or compost to boost its fertility.

Draining Capacity: The rate at which water drains from your soil determines its health. For example, if water drains slowly from the soil, it can cause waterlogging or root rot, whereas if it drains too quickly, it can wash nutrients off the soil or dry out too quickly.

Soil Looseness: The looseness of the soil means that there is enough air in the soil to boost growth. Oxygen is made available to the roots, and other microorganisms living in the soil can survive and produce nutrients for plant growth and development.

Soil pH Value: The soil's acidity or alkalinity significantly impacts your garden's survival and productivity. While some plants require a pH of 5.5 to 6.5 to thrive, others require nutrients that can only be absorbed in different pH levels. This is why you need to test your soil carefully before you choose a spot for your garden.

Depth of the Soil: To determine the soil depth you intend to use in your garden, dig test holes in various places and measure their depths to decide which to use. Some soils require digging as deep as 5 ft. before you reach bedrock, whereas others do not. Some are as shallow as one foot, so you should work out how much topsoil you have before deciding where to put your garden. Even though most plants can adapt to shallow soil, deep soils are preferable for planting your garden.

3. Availability of Water

Mulch and compost help your soil retain water and resist drought, but they do not eliminate the need to water your garden regularly. Your plants need enough water so your seeds can germinate, and they continue to require water as they grow to stay healthy and produce optimally. This is why you need a steady supply of water near your garden in addition to a hose long enough to facilitate distribution.

4. Accessibility

You should place your garden in an area that is easily accessible to both you and anyone who manages it for you. Easy access means you can get to the garden and tend to it as needed; you can visit it whenever you want to fumigate, water, or weed it. It means you can move your gardening equipment around freely and without restriction and bring in compost as needed without trampling on your garden's plants. You'll get more done and enjoy tending to your garden and harvests if you can get to them quickly and easily.

It would be best if you also considered how accessible your garden is to other elements, both positive and negative. For example, how does rainwater flow through your garden? Is there adequate drainage to channel water from rain or snowmelt to avoid flooding or waterlogging? What kind of access does the wind have in your garden? Will the wind bring dirt and other unwanted items from the surrounding environment into your garden? What about animals?

Do they have free access to and from your garden? If they do, your garden is in jeopardy.

5. Other Trees and Shrubs

Your garden should be located in an area free of other trees and shrubs so that they do not compete with it for soil and other nutrients. If trees shade the garden, it may not receive the full benefit of solar nutrients. At the same time, the roots of surrounding trees and shrubs can spread far from where they are planted and encroach on the garden's undersoil, competing for nutrients with the garden.

6. General Design of the Community

When planning the location of your garden, consider the possibility of new structures surrounding your garden in the future. The appropriate authority in charge of town planning should make this information available. When choosing a location for your garden, keep utility lines in mind.

You should ensure that no new house is built close to your garden that will cast shadows on it, preventing the sun from reaching it. Consider whether larger and taller trees will grow nearby and suffocate the nutrients in your garden. With all these factors considered, you can be confident that your garden will last long in its current location.

7. Free Flow of Air

When choosing a place for your garden, you should think about how well it gets air because plants need enough air to live and grow. The more air circulates through your garden, the less you will battle fungus, mold, and other moisture-dependent diseases.

8. Free of Contaminations

Your garden's location should be free of pollution and contamination from any possible toxic waste from industry. You might have to deal with such contamination if the site was previously used for commercial or industrial purposes.

9. Flat Surface

Plant your garden on a slope or hill to avoid being washed away by a flood. With a flat surface, you don't have to fight erosion, which lowers the cost of running and taking care of the garden.

10. Opportunity for Expansion

When planning your garden location, consider whether it has the potential to accommodate future growth. This is because, as you gain experience with growing plants for tea making, you may want to expand your garden by adding new fruits, shrubs, or vegetables. You don't want to relocate your garden too frequently or separate them from each other because this will be inconvenient.

11. Protection

Build your garden in an easy-to-protect location. Choose a site not prone to rodent attacks that feed on tomatoes, carrots, and vegetables. Use proper fencing methods like wire mesh or iron fencing to protect your garden from attacks by these pests. While building fences for security, dig some way down to protect your garden from underground varmints. Protect your garden from toxic insecticides and pesticides that could harm it as well.

12. Hardiness Factor

The hardiness factor refers to a plant's ability to thrive in cold temperatures and withstand wind, heat, flooding, and drought. So, it would be best if you used a place that is not too prone to factors that could unnecessarily need your plants to be hardy.

13. Workload Involved

Consider how much time you will devote to managing your garden due to its location. You may need to create a garden bed in your chosen space, weed out grasses and tear up topsoil, dig out roots and rocks, amend the soil if necessary, and build fences on and underneath the soil.

Spacing for a Tea Garden

Teas have recently been planted to allow for more plants per square meter, as opposed to what was previously possible when they were planted 150 to 180 cm apart. Once, they were planted in square forms, but now, diagonal and triangular patterns are common, resulting in more teas being accommodated.

Fertility of the soil, availability of water, and availability of growth-promoting factors are all issues that influence the pattern and arrangement of planting tea.

A tea garden's ideal plant population is between 14,000 and 18,000 plants per hectare, as anything above this may result in overcrowding. As a beginner, however, you may simply keep this knowledge while building at your own pace. While this recommendation promotes quick ground coverage and early yield, you can use it as a yardstick to work out how much space you have in relation to your plants. This will help you decide how to space your tea garden. Also, you must ensure you plant them on a flat surface where you will not have to deal with any water damage, such as erosion.

How to Grow a Tea Garden on a Roof

One method for growing a tea garden on your roof is to convert your entire roof into a garden. The procedures for accomplishing this are as follows:

- First, waterproof the roof to prevent leaks or water dripping down the building. Make certain that it is frost-resistant and long-lasting.

- The protection layer, which protects the roof from moisture and temperature fluctuations, is then installed using PIR panels, PS extruded polystyrene boards or polyurethane foam. This also strengthens the roof and increases its durability.

- The drainage layer follows, which aids in removing rainwater from the plants by channeling it to the drainage in the roof and then away.

- Then, add the geotextile layer, which separates the plant-growing layer from the drainage layer. It aids in sieving soil and other particles from the drainage layer, preventing it from becoming clogged and causing waterlogging.

- Install the vegetation layer, which contains the soil for your plants to grow. It should have adequate air circulation and water permeability.

How to Grow a Tea Garden on a Balcony

Growing a tea garden on your balcony might be as easy as using flower pots or baskets with lids you already have.

The pots should be kept securely on the balcony and properly cared for.

Wash and dry the products before planting them in a flower pot and watering them regularly.

Alternatively, you can grow your garden with store-bought seeds.

Using the above considerations, you can create an ideal environment for your seed to grow quickly and produce optimally.

How to Grow Tea in a Garden

To grow tea in a garden, decide where in your garden you want to grow tea and prepare it properly.

Prepare your soil and ensure it is suitable for your tea plants. Weed thoroughly and turn the topsoil to mix the nutrients.

Then, build a box for your herb garden and make sure it gets enough sunlight. You will still need to fertilize your herbs as they grow and weed them as required.

Choose herbs that complement one another so they do not compete for nutrients. Different mint plants, lemon balm paired with bee balm, and lemon verbena paired with lavender are complementary plants to consider.

How to Grow Tea Garden in a Container

- Tea garden built-in containers should have root balls roughly half the size of the pot used to plant them, and the pot should have numerous drainage holes.

- Fill the pot with soil until it is one-third full.

- Place the plant on the soil and cover it with soil, leaving the bulb exposed.

- Keep the pot in a well-lit area with a temperature above 270°C.

- Provide enough water to the plant, but not too much, to avoid waterlogging.

- Water the plant until it drains through the holes in the pots.

- Allow it to drain, and ensure the pot is not submerged.

- Introduce fertilizers as the plant grows.

How to Grow Tea Garden in a Raised Bed

Think about where the sun will be coming from before you start planting in raised beds; you don't want your larger plants to block the sunlight for the plants in the back. It would help if you positioned your tea plants to get at least five and preferably six hours of sunshine each day.

When spreading seeds or planting seedlings, thoroughly study the seed package or plant tag to understand what conditions the tea plants need to grow.

Consider the following if you want to grow anything other than tea plants in your garden:

When seeding other plants, like vegetables, follow the thinning instructions once the sprouts begin to poke through the soil. Beet sprouts, for instance, may be kept and used in a salad.

In contrast, carrot seedlings need to be buried when they first appear. Root crops like beets, carrots, radishes, and turnips benefit from thinning to promote strong root development and increase harvest size.

Choosing where to plant your garden requires you to consider every factor involved in the growth and productivity of your garden. Nature has provided some factors that make plant growth and productivity possible and easy. You are responsible for using these natural elements to your advantage when deciding where to set up your garden.

The next step is to assess soil health, which includes measuring the pH of the soil, its fertility, looseness, drainage capacity, and depth. In addition, consider water availability, accessibility, and the proximity of other trees and shrubs to your garden site.

You must also inspect the level of aeration and ensure that there are no chemical or industrial waste contaminants. Ensure the surface is flat and not sloppy to avoid erosion; consider the workload involved in managing your garden at the site you've chosen and put in place the necessary protective measures to keep rodents and other threats at bay.

Chapter 4

Plant Index

There are many plants that you can grow in a tea garden. Your choice depends on the climate conditions of the area you live in, the space available for your garden, the flavor you like, and the medical benefit you need from the plants. This chapter lists the most essential plants to grow for tea, along with comprehensive instructions on how to plant them. You can use them fresh or dry, and some of them have several parts you can use, including flowers, seeds, leaves, and fruits. For beginners, it's recommended to plant herbs that you'll frequently use. After planting, you'll need to wait until the plant matures enough to remove any parts. This particularly applies to the leaves, which many new gardeners are tempted to remove too soon, deriving the plants from their ability to perform photosynthesis and thrive. Besides planting, you'll need to be careful about the upkeep, including watering and fertilizing.

Rosemary

Although rosemary is prevalently used as an herb in Mediterranean-style dishes, its soothing fragrance makes it perfect for teas. It has plenty of health benefits, from aiding digestion to relieving symptoms of stress and anxiety. You can grow rosemary in any corner of your home, and you'll have plenty of leaves to put into the teapot all year around. Rosemary can be propagated from the seed or root and stem cuttings. Several types of rosemary are divided into two main categories - trailing varieties and upright plants.

Instructions:

1. If you're planting in pots, start by choosing the proper size container. You'll need a medium to large container to cultivate upright varieties, while trailing forms can grow in smaller pots. In any case, the container should be at least 6 inches deep. Choose pots made from material that absorbs any excess moisture, as rosemary doesn't tolerate high soil humidity. Terra-cotta pots work the best.

2. If you're planting in an outdoor garden, skip the first step and start by preparing the soil. Don't use garden soil as it's too dense for rosemary. Buy or make your own soil mix to create light soil with good drainage. Add 20% of compost to enrich it with nutrients to give the cuttings or seeds a good start for the propagation process.

3. Select the perfect spot for your rosemary. Whether they're growing indoors or outdoors, these plants should receive at least six hours of direct sunlight during the day. If you live in a tropical climate, place the rosemary in a light shade. If you're growing the plant indoors, place the pot in a south-facing area.

4. If you're growing from seeds, all you need to do is fill the pot about halfway with the soil, put in the seeds, and cover them with soil. It takes a lot of time for the plant to grow to the appropriate size, so this method is rarely recommended.

5. If you're propagating from cuttings, you'll need a few young but mature shoots without flowers. If you're cutting them from the existing plant, make sure you cut the shoots 3-4 inches long. If you're buying the cuttings, only purchase healthy ones that are the appropriate size.

6. Take a sharp knife or shears to remove the leaves from the bottom of the cuttings. Leave only leaves at the top half inches of the shoot.

7. Dip the end without the leaves into a plant growth hormone and place it into the soil. The use of hormones is optional, but it speeds up the growth process of cutting considerably.

8. Water the soil lightly and wait until the top two inches of the soil dry out before watering it again. Fertilize with liquid fertilizer in 3-4 weeks.

Lavender

Lavender is another easy plant to grow - and since it's a perennial, you can renew it each year. Its purple flowers and muted green foliage will provide the perfect soothing fragrance to your garden and teas. Plant this herb in early spring after the last frost has gone, and you'll be able to keep it outdoors until the following winter. Harvest and dry the leaves and the flowers when they mature and prepare teas for pain and anxiety relief. Depending on your climate conditions, you can grow three varieties of lavender. These are English (loves moderate to war climate), Spanish (grows in Mediterranean climate), and French lavender (doesn't tolerate temperature changes).

Instructions:

1. Begin preparing the cuttings by separating a healthy, mature shoot from the main stem. When planting in the spring, you'll use flexible softwood cuttings. If you have a small indoor tea garden, use hardwood cuttings. These are available in the fall and take longer to grow. Cut hardwood shoots below the leaf node.

2. Choose the spot for your lavender. Avoid planting in the shade, as this prevents the leaves from growing and creating fragrant oils. The best temperature range to grow lavender is 68-86°F - pick the spot where this range can be maintained.

3. Create the proper soil mixture. Add a handful of sand for each pot/plant to ensure the soil has good draining to avoid creating a waterlogged medium when watering your plants. If the medium requires it, add a small amount of organic fertilizer. The growth medium should be slightly alkaline (pH between 6 and 7) to ensure optimal growth conditions for the cuttings.

4. Using an herb stripper, remove the leaves from the bottom of the cuttings and place them into the soil. Cover the bottom with the soil mixture and water lightly.

5. If you've planted in a pot, cover the container with a plastic bag and place it in an area where it will receive at least six hours of filtered sunlight. If you're planting in an outdoor garden, cover only the cuttings or place them in a small greenhouse.

6. Depending on the climate, softwood cuttings will root in 2-4 weeks, while hardwood shoots will take root in 5-6 weeks.

7. Wait until the topsoil becomes dry to the touch before watering again, but don't let the entire medium dry out completely.

8. If you added a small amount of organic fertilizer at the time of the planting, wait at least 6 weeks before applying liquid fertilizer. If you haven't added organic matter at planting, add some when the cuttings start to root and 6 weeks after that.

Roses

Roses are known for creating a beautiful sight and a lingering soft fragrance in the garden. They also have plenty of health benefits. You can brew tea from fresh and dry rose petals, depending on the aroma you like. Use it to reduce inflammatory reactions, blood sugar levels, and blood pressure or boost cognitive functions. If you live in an area with a moderate to cold climate, push the propagation to early summer. Within Mediterranean, tropical, and subtropical climates, spring has the optimal temperature for blooming roses. If you're planting indoors, you can also propagate them in fall or early winter.

1. If you're planting in pots, start by picking out a medium to large container. To give your cutting the best start, propagate them a few days apart and use several sizes of containers. This will help you avoid overgrowth happening too soon. Skip this step if you're planting in an outdoor garden.

2. For smaller varieties, you'll need a space that has a diameter of 8-12 inches, while larger roses need 14-18 in diameter for optimal growth. Be sure to pay attention to this when planting, regardless of whether you do it in the garden or pots, to avoid overcrowding.

3. Buy or make the right soil mixture. Roses don't require fertilizer at planting, but they need plenty of organic matter. You can use any type of soil available. Just make sure it's well-draining and mix it with plenty of hummus.

4. Choose the spot for the roses. At the beginning of growth, roses should be kept sheltered and only receive a few hours of light, filtered sunlight.

5. Prepare your stems. If you've bought plants already in soil, they can go directly to your soil mixture. If you've purchased bare root stems, dip them into a bowl of water for 1-2 hours. By allowing them to absorb more moisture, you're giving them a better chance of adapting to their new environment.

6. Place the stems into the soil, water them thoroughly and ensure they don't receive much sunlight for at least a week. You can cover them if necessary. After that, they should be exposed to 5-7 hours of direct but moderate sunlight.

7. Check them frequently after planting. If you live in a warmer climate, you'll need to replenish to water very soon because roses don't like to be dry when starting to root.

8. Two to three weeks after the planting, you can apply the first batch of liquid fertilizer. If needed, add some manure or compost as well.

Raspberry

Raspberry leaves can be just as delicious in teas as the fruit of this plant is in desserts. The ideal time for gathering raspberry leaves is right after you've picked the last of the fruit in fall. Around this time, they're full of soothing agents, which are good for pain relief and against bloating. The best time to propagate raspberry is early spring, but you can also plant it in the fall and, if you're growing in a pot, even in early winter. Propagation can be done from bare root plants and cuttings from potted plants. The latter provides quicker results and is available all year round. Whereas the former is only sold during the winter. You'll need to plant them as soon as you get them.

Instructions:

1. If you're planting in a pot, find containers 16-20 inches in diameter. It should have drainage holes in the base for the

excess water. If you're planting in the garden, leave the same amount of room for each plant (a perimeter of 16-20 inches in diameter around them).

2. Raspberries require plenty of daylight, so choose a place where they'll be exposed to 6-8 hours of direct sunlight. Make sure it isn't too windy - as this could cause the soil to dry out too quickly; if you live in a moderate to warm climate, plant the raspberries away from direct sunlight.

3. Mix the soil. This plant requires ample organic matter to thrive. Otherwise, it won't fruit, and the leaves will lack the beneficial ingredient you need in tea. The medium needs to be only slightly acidic (pH of 6.2-6.7), rich in fertilizer, and well-draining. You can buy a premade potting mix for berries or make your own by adding compost (or humus) and aged manure into light soil. If you only have heavy soil available, buying a commercial mix is a more economical solution.

4. Bare-rooted cuttings should be soaked in water before going into the soil. Whereas cuttings from a plotted plant can be planted directly after cutting. If you're using the latter, cut the shoot with a clean tool and remove the bottom leaves before putting it into the soil.

5. Once the raspberries are planted, water the soil moderately without making the soil water clogged. If you're keeping the

plants in a bright place, you'll have to wait again in a day or two. Check the topsoil - if it's dry, you can water it again.

6. Keep the plants in the temperature range of 60-80 F and fertilize them again after 4-6 weeks. Avoid using fresh manure because it can add a strange flavor to the fruit and leaves.

Strawberry

Similarly, to raspberries, strawberries are also easy plants to grow. Not only that, but you'll need even less space. They do well in everything from hanging baskets to pots and window boxes to outdoor garden beds. And just as with raspberry leaves, strawberry leaves are also a great addition to teas. Depending on the space available, you'll need to choose whether to cultivate perennial or annual strawberry plants. Depending on your growing environment, you can also choose from three different varieties. If planting in a garden in a climate with big temperature fluctuations, you should opt for the day-neutral variant. This one does well in most temperature conditions. If you live in a warm climate, you should get the ever-bearing variety, which fruits twice a year. However, if you're growing strawberries in small pots, you should get a June bearer, which bears once, leaving more time for the leaves to absorb the nutrients from the limited space. There are several ways to propagate strawberries: through runners (roots with leaves developed by the plant), stored runners (runners separated from the mother plant and stored in cold conditions), misted tips (the top part of the mother plant), and potted plants.

1. After choosing the planting method that suits you and your climate, pick the location. The plant should receive 5-6 hours of direct sunlight a day and be sheltered from the wind.

2. Prepare well-drained soil. Strawberries need acidic soil. You can obtain this by mixing organic matter into commercial, all-purpose soil (if you're planting in pots). Or make it by incorporating plenty of compost, coffee grounds, and other organic material into regular garden soil.

3. If planting in the garden, place the strawberries in raised beds, leaving a 16 to 18-inch space between the plants. If growing in pots, the containers should have this diameter and be placed at least 3-4 feet apart. While the plants go smaller than raspberries, they often develop multiple runners, which can create a mess if the plants are planted too close to each other.

4. Place the strawberries or runners into the soil medium. The soil shouldn't cover the crown and the leaves. This is crucial for having upright plants, which can absorb more sunlight and become nutrient dense.

5. Water thoroughly and check frequently after the first watering. If you live in a warmer climate, you'll need to water your strawberries at least every two days. As the plant

takes root and develops its mature leaves, it will need even more water.

6. Fertilize the plants when they start to develop and use potassium-rich liquid fertilizer to give the leaves, flowers, and fruit a good start.

Tea Plant

If you live in a subtropical or tropical climate, you'll be able to grow tea easily and have plenty of it stored for your daily tea needs. The tea plant has an incredible invigorating effect, yet, at the same time, it relieves symptoms of anxiety and stress. The original tea plant is a hardy perennial green, which yields plenty of leaves all year round. You can propagate this plant anytime during the year, indoors or outdoors. Make sure the temperatures are not scorching hot or freezing. Otherwise, your tea plant won't grow. Propagation is possible from seeds and cuttings, but you can also get tea plants from a nursery. If you want to grow but don't want to wait too much until the plant is ready to harvest plant cuttings.

Instructions:
1. After choosing a suitable planting method, find the right spot for the tea plant. It loves partial shade and moderate sunlight. Whether you're planting in a container or in the garden, avoid placing tea in too warm or windy places, as these will hinder its growth.

2. If you're a container grower, you'll need to find pots 6-8 inches in diameter for new tea plants, while mature tea needs larger containers.

3. Tea thrives in slightly acidic soil (with a pH between 4.5 and 5.6). If you're planting in your garden, check the acidity of your soil. If the acidity of the medium is not within the required range, adding pine needles and sulfur should lower its pH level.

4. Depending on the form of planting you've chosen, place the cuttings, plants, or seeds and cover them (partially cover the former two and the latter fully).

5. Water the soil until it becomes moist to the touch but not soaked through. Check on it regularly to ensure the topsoil never dries out fully.

6. Tea plants rarely require fertilizer. However, if your plant doesn't grow properly, give it a boost with a little nitrogen-rich fertilizer. Make sure to do this at least 8 weeks after planting.

Mint

You can't have a tea garden without planting a true staple like mint. Mint is one of the most versatile herbs you can cultivate. It's fragrant fresh, or dry and has plenty of beneficial bioactive compounds. There are plenty of varieties to choose from - with peppermint and spearmint being the most common ones. Chocolate mint is also popular, and, like all mint varieties, it's quick to grow indoors or outdoors. Choose the variety depending on the flavors you like and the benefits you need. Some are better for digestion issues, while others soothe the nervous system. Propagation is just as easy from cutting as it is from runners, but you can pick whichever method you prefer.

Instructions:

1. If you're propagating from cutting, start by cutting healthy shoots with a clean and sharp tool. Place the cuttings in the water and wait until they develop roots. If using runners, you already have the beginning of the root system and can start from step 2.

2. Choose the perfect spot for growing mint. The plant lives indirect sunlight. If you're planting indoors, put it in a room with an east-facing window. If cultivating outdoors, plant the mint in a shade of a tree to protect it from the harsh afternoon sun in the summer.

3. Mint loves enriched and well-draining potting mixes and garden soils. Incorporating plenty of organic matter into the medium when planting gives your plants a good start. Make your own mint-friendly soil mix by combining 1 part sterile garden soil, 1 part Sterile, and 1 part peat moss - or by a commercial one. You can even place a layer of aged manure or compost onto the surface of the soil right after planting.

4. Transfer the cuttings or runners into the soil. If you're planning in containers, these should be 6-8 inches deep and as wide as your space allows. They should have adequate drainage holes. If planting in the garden, leave enough space between the plants as mint spreads quickly and will develop plenty of runners.

5. Water the soil after planting moderately, and regularly check to ensure it stays moist. Whenever the topsoil becomes dry to the touch, replenish the water. However, be careful not to overwater it, as this can cause the mint to become waterlogged and die.

6. Mint doesn't require much fertilizer. If you need to add some, use water-soluble liquid fertilizer to ensure the plants thrive without losing their flavor.

Chapter 5

Preserving the Harvest

Around the world, people have been harvesting plants to manufacture tea for ages. Making herbal teas from wild plants is a wonderful way to enjoy the healing properties of herbal infusions while bringing nature into your house.

The harvest season for tea is a critical time of year. It's the moment when all of a year's hard work comes together to be enjoyed.

Therefore, it is essential that the tea harvesting process is performed correctly and with great care. In this chapter, we will explore how to preserve tea harvest.

Firstly, preserving the tea harvest means ensuring that only high-quality leaves, seeds, fruits, and vegetables are harvested to make a top-notch cup of tea. When these parts are harvested at their peak ripeness, they contain more flavor components such as polyphenols, tannins, amino acids, sugars, and other compounds that give tea its unique taste and character. The flavor and aroma can be adversely affected if the plant parts are harvested too early or too late.

Finally, preserving your harvest also ensures a steady supply of tea for everyone to enjoy.

Preserving the tea harvest is an undertaking that protects our environment, supports sustainable farming practices, and guarantees a steady supply of top-quality teas. Tea connoisseurs know the importance of managing a tea harvest from one's own garden to preserve the unique taste of the leaves. Though the process appears complicated, with a few tips, anyone can grow and store quality teas right in their backyard. With careful attention given to each step and thoughtful consideration of the relevant elements, you can transform your home-grown tea crop into something amazing.

Harvesting Leaves

Harvesting the leaves of a plant to make tea is a simple yet rewarding activity. It can provide an enjoyable experience that involves being outdoors and engaging with nature. Here are step-by-step instructions to help you harvest the perfect leaves for your tea.

Step 1: Choosing your plant - The first step in harvesting leaves for making tea is selecting the appropriate type of plant. Depending on your preference, different varieties of plants can be suitable for making tea, such as chamomile, hibiscus, or lavender. Do the research and find out which type of plant grows in your area and produces good-quality leaves for making tea.

Step 2: Timing the harvest -Once you have chosen the plant, you will need to consider when to harvest. Generally, harvesting should be done in the morning when the leaves are still full of moisture. This is because as the day progresses and temperatures increase, the oils inside the leaves start evaporating.

Step 3: Collecting leaves - After deciding on the right time to harvest, you can now go out into your garden or nearby area and collect some leaves. You should be careful not to damage any part of the plant while collecting. Make sure that you only pick off mature and healthy-looking leaves, as these will give you a better quality tea.

Step 4: Drying leaves - Once you have collected enough leaves, they must be dried before being used for tea. You can do this by spreading out the leaves on a flat surface, making sure that air can circulate around them. This should be done in a cool, dry place with good ventilation. Leave the leaves to dry for approximately one week or until they become brittle.

Step 5: Store leaves - Once your leaves have been dried, you need to store them properly so they retain their flavor and aroma when brewed into tea. Place the dried leaves in an airtight container such as a jar and store it away from direct sunlight or heat sources such as stoves or ovens.

Now that you have followed these steps to harvest and store your own leaves, you are ready to make some delicious tea! Enjoy your homemade tea and the satisfaction of knowing that you made it from your own freshly harvested leaves.

Harvesting Seeds

Harvesting seeds for tea is a wonderful way to enjoy the benefits of plants in a natural and delicious way. To succeed when harvesting these seeds, a few essential steps need to be followed.

Step 1: Select your plant – The best type of plant to harvest depends on what type of tea you want. For example, if you are looking for an herbal tea, then choose plants such as chamomile, mint, or lemon balm, which have known soothing properties. Other popular plants for teas include peppermint, rosehips, and hibiscus.

Step 2: Prepare the plant – Before harvesting any seed pods or flowers, ensure that the plant is completely clean and healthy. Before harvesting the seeds, check for any signs of pests or disease and remove any affected parts.

Step 3: Harvest the seeds – Once you have selected your plant and prepared it, you can now begin to harvest the seeds. Depending on the type of plant that you are harvesting from, this can involve picking seed pods or flowers. Make sure that only ripe seed pods are harvested, as these will contain mature and viable seeds which will be suitable for making tea.

Step 4: Dry the seeds – The next step is to dry out the harvested seeds so they can be stored safely until they are ready to be used in a tea blend. Place the harvested flowers or seed pods on a paper towel and leave them in a warm, dry place for several days. Once they have dried out completely, store the seeds in an airtight container.

Step 5: Make the tea – Now that you have harvested and dried your seeds, you are ready to make your tea. To do this, measure out the desired amount of seeds into a teapot or cup and pour boiling water over it. Allow it to steep for around five minutes before straining off the liquid and enjoying your homemade tea!

Harvesting seeds from plants is a great way to enjoy their unique properties in a delicious cup of tea. By following these steps, you can ensure that you get the most out of your harvest and enjoy some truly special teas.

Harvesting Flowers

Harvesting flowers to make tea is one of the most rewarding and enjoyable gardening activities. Not only can you enjoy a delicious herbal beverage, but you also have the chance to get up close and personal with nature as you collect various types of blooms from your garden or local area.

Here are step-by-step instructions on how to harvest flowers for tea:

Step 1: Prepare your harvest site –Choose an area that is dry, away from direct sunlight, and free of dust, dirt, and pesticides. If desired, set up a tarp or clean surface to collect your flowers.

Step 2: Collect your flowers – Gently pick the blossoms with your fingertips or use small scissors to snip them off. Collect only the flowers you plan to use to make your tea, as they should be used fresh.

Step 3: Remove any leaves or stems – Separate any foliage, stems, or bugs from the flowers before using them. Rinse gently with water if needed, then lay out the flowers on a clean surface and let air dry for several hours.

Step 4: Dry your flowers – If you don't have time for air-drying, place your flowers between two paper towels and press gently to remove excess moisture. You can also dry your harvest in an oven set to a low temperature (140F/60C) for about 15 minutes. Once dried, store in an airtight container in a cool, dark place.

Step 5: Make your tea – To make tea, pour boiling water over 2-3 teaspoons of dried flowers and steep for 3-5 minutes. Strain before serving. You can also mix different types of flowers together to create your own unique herbal blend!

Harvesting flowers for tea is simple and fun! With just a few steps, you can bring the beauty of nature into your home and enjoy a delicious cup of herbal refreshment. Enjoy!

Harvesting Fruits

Harvesting fruits to make tea is one of the oldest methods of brewing a cup of tea. There are many types of tea that can be made from harvested fruits, such as blackberry, strawberry, raspberry, elderberry, blueberry, and more. The process of harvesting and making these types of teas requires careful preparation.

The first step in harvesting fruits for tea is selecting the right type of fruit. You want to pick a fruit that has not been exposed to pesticides or chemicals, so it is vital to source your harvest sustainably. Each type of fruit has its right time for harvesting, so you will need to know the optimal time of year when the fruit is ripe and ready for harvesting. Depending on your location and climate, this can vary greatly.

Once you have selected the type of fruit you want to harvest, it is essential to do so in a methodical way. It is advisable to wear gloves when handling fruit as it keeps them clean, protects your hands from cuts or scratches, and prevents contamination from any other substances on your hands. When harvesting, select fruits that are ripe enough but still firm, as these will taste better and keep longer when stored. Once harvested, place the fruits into containers carefully so they don't get squashed or bruised during transport home.

When making tea with fruits, the next step is to prepare the fruit. Depending on the type of fruit you have chosen, there are different ways of preparing them for tea. For example, if making strawberry or raspberry tea, use a sieve to press the juice out from the flesh without releasing any seeds into the liquid. For blackberry and blueberry teas, simply add one part water to two parts of mashed fruit and heat until it starts simmering in order to extract all of its flavorful juices.

Once you have prepared your infusion base (either by pressing or heating), it is time to steep your tea. You can leave your fruits steeping for up to 10 minutes, depending on how strong a cup you would like but consider that leaving it longer can lead to a bitter taste. When steeping, make sure the temperature of your tea is not too hot, as this can burn and destroy some of the flavors in the fruit. Once it has reached the right temperature (usually around 70-80 degrees Celsius), remove from heat and let it steep for 5-10 minutes.

When finished steeping, strain out any clots of fruit or sediment and pour them into cups. You can sweeten with honey if desired, but usually, these types of teas are naturally sweet, so taste before adding additional elements to determine if necessary. Enjoy your homemade tea.

Harvesting fruits to make tea is a simple process that allows you to enjoy fresh, natural flavors without needing to buy expensive commercial products. Follow these step-by-step instructions, and you will be able to harvest different types of fruits and make your own delicious teas in no time.

Harvesting Vegetables

Making tea from freshly harvested vegetables is an easy way to get the most out of your garden. With a few simple steps, you can make a delicious cup of vegetable tea with all the benefits of fresh-picked produce without added chemicals or preservatives. Below are the steps on how to harvest vegetables for tea.

First, choose the right time to harvest. The best time to pick vegetables for tea depends on what type you are growing. Leafy greens such as lettuce and spinach should be picked when they are young and tender, while root crops like carrots and potatoes should be harvested when they reach their full size. In general, it's best to harvest vegetables in the early morning while they are still cool and crisp.

Once you've chosen the right time to pick your produce, it's time to start harvesting. The most important thing is to use clean, sharp tools when cutting or pulling vegetables from their plants. Knives should be sharpened before each use, and make sure that there are no jagged edges on the tools that can cause damage to the plants or vegetables. When harvesting root crops like carrots, turnips, and potatoes, pull gently so as not to damage them. It's best to start by loosening the soil around the vegetable with a garden fork first before attempting to pull it out of the ground.

After you've harvested all the vegetables for your tea, it's time to prepare them. Start by washing them thoroughly in cold water to remove any dirt or debris. Then, chop and dice into small pieces depending on how you plan to use them. For most herbal teas, smaller pieces are better as they will infuse faster into hot water.

Once your vegetables are prepared, put them into a pot of boiling water and let simmer for 10-15 minutes until the desired strength is reached. If desired, add a sweetener such as honey or sugar for an added touch of sweetness. Once finished brewing, strain out the vegetables and enjoy your freshly brewed cup of vegetable tea.

Harvesting vegetables for tea is an easy year-round activity. Whether you are harvesting from your own garden or buying fresh produce from the market, taking the time to make tea with freshly harvested vegetables is an excellent way to get the most out of your vegetables.

Importance of Preserving the Harvest

When it comes to tea gardens, the importance of preserving the harvest cannot be overstated. A great cup of tea begins with a properly selected harvest, which means that properly preserved tea is essential for ensuring a quality product. Tea leaves that are allowed to decay will not produce the same flavor as freshly-harvested, carefully preserved leaves. Not only does preserving the harvested tea allow farmers to maintain consistent standards in their products, but it also helps to maximize good harvest by preventing loss due to spoilage or other deterioration. Properly storing harvested tea leaves can also help extend their shelf life, meaning fewer costly replacements and allowing farmers to focus their efforts on sustainable farming practices. Preserving the harvest from your tea garden can prove to be incredibly beneficial in terms of maintaining quality and profitability in the future.

Preserving tea harvested from a home's tea garden is essential for its nutritional and medicinal value and aesthetic beauty. It can be used to make multiple cups of comforting tea, but the harvesting process itself is quite enjoyable. Aside from that, here are some other key benefits of preserving tea from your home personal tea garden:

1. **Cost Savings:** Preserving tea from a home garden is often much cheaper than buying pre-packaged teas in stores. You save on the costs of buying individual bags or sachets and shipping fees for having the product delivered to you. Plus, you won't have to worry about wasting money on unnecessary packaging materials or artificial preservatives that are often found in store-bought varieties.

2. **Unique Taste:** Home-grown teas may have different flavors than what can be found at the store due to the type of soil where grown, climate conditions, and age of leaves when harvested. It is a great way to experiment with new flavor profiles and find something unique that will surprise and delight your taste buds!

3. **Health Benefits:** Tea harvested from your garden contains higher levels of antioxidants than those bought in stores because they have not gone through any chemical processing or storage procedures that can break down some of these beneficial compounds over time. As such, freshly harvested teas may provide greater health benefits when consumed regularly, such as improved digestion, increased energy levels, and better immunity against illnesses.

4. **Conservation of Resources:** When preserving home-grown teas for future use, you are conserving natural resources - like water - which would otherwise go into producing store-bought teas that require large amounts of resources before reaching their final destination. Additionally, this reduces our environmental impact by decreasing the demand for plastic packaging materials and carbon emissions generated from transportation methods associated with purchasing pre-packaged products from retailers located far away from our homes.

5. **Sustainability and Self-Sufficiency:** By growing your own herbs for harvesting and storing them for later use, you are

taking steps towards greater self-sufficiency while creating a more sustainable lifestyle in general – all without sacrificing flavor or quality! This also helps support local agriculture while saving money since many common grocery items are usually much pricier than what they cost when purchased directly from farmers or markets near you!

Methods for Preserving the Harvest

Preserving the harvest is a crucial task for any gardener to ensure that your products and goods can be used throughout the year. There are many different methods, and each has its own advantages and disadvantages.

The first method of preservation is pickling. Pickling uses salt and acidic liquids, such as vinegar or lemon juice, to seal moisture from the food, so it does not spoil. This process also adds flavor to food, making them more flavorful than fresh produce. The downside to this method is that it requires preparation time, but it preserves foods longer than other methods.

Canning is another popular way to preserve food. Canning involves sealing food items in airtight containers, either with a canning machine or by boiling the container in water. This method prevents bacteria from growing, helps keep food safe for extended storage, and locks in flavor and nutrients.

Freezing is another common method of preserving the harvest. Freezing preserves food by preventing bacterial growth and retaining the flavor and texture of fresh produce. The downside to this is that it requires electricity or gas-powered freezers, as well as careful packaging to prevent freezer burn on foods.

Dehydrating is a process that removes moisture from fruits and vegetables through either air drying or using a dehydrator machine. This method results in concentrated flavors and vitamins, making them ideal for snacks such as dried fruit leathers or chips made out of vegetables. It is also a great way to store herbs and spices.

Smoking is another method of preserving the harvest, involving using smoke from wood chips or pellets, usually in a smoker machine. Smoking keeps food safe for longer storage periods and adds flavor to meats and other items.

Lastly, curing is a method that uses salt, sugar, vinegar, and/or nitrates to preserve food. This process helps prevent bacterial growth by extracting moisture from food and adds flavor and texture. Curing is commonly used on meats such as bacon or ham.

No matter what methods one chooses for preserving the harvest, it's critical that one use safe practices such as proper packaging materials, sealed containers, and cool and dry places for storage. Taking these precautions ensures that their harvest will be safe and flavorful to enjoy throughout the year. With all of these methods, as well as careful preparation and storage methods, gardeners can extend the life of their products so they can enjoy it year-round.

Chapter 6

Dealing with Diseased Plants

Tea plantations worldwide are vulnerable to various diseases and pests, which can wreak havoc on the tea plants themselves. Although some may appear minor, these issues can quickly escalate to cause significant harm if not dealt with promptly. If you're a tea grower, it's essential that you monitor your garden for signs of disease and act quickly to stop the issue from spreading. Several methods are available to deal with diseased tea plants, from controlling soil-borne fungal diseases with vigilant sanitation techniques to fighting viral infestations using effective pruning techniques. With regular observation of your plants complemented by timely treatments tailored to your unique conditions, you can mitigate any risk caused by diseases and restore your garden's health in no time.

Diseases That Can Damage Your Tea Plants

1. Algal Leaf Spot

Algal Leaf Spot Disease is a common problem for many tea plants worldwide. It is caused by the fungus Cephaleuros virescens and can be identified by its yellowish-green or olive-green color spots found on the leaves of the tea plant. These spots are 1-3mm in diameter and occur in circular clusters. The disease may also affect the stems and twigs of a tea plant, resulting in the lightening or darkening of the bark. The infection can spread rapidly if not managed properly, causing significant damage to your tea plants.

To identify algal leaf spot disease on your tea plants, look out for the yellowish-green or olive-green circular spots. Additionally, white powdery films may also be present around the spots on infected tea leaves. If left untreated, these infected leaves will eventually drop from the plant.

To help prevent an outbreak of algal leaf spot disease, it is vital to practice proper sanitation and control measures such as removing affected leaves and branches and avoiding overhead irrigation. It is also crucial to avoid overcrowding tea plants as this can increase the risk of spreading the disease.

To treat algal leaf spot, you should first remove any affected leaves or branches from the plant. Next, spray the entire plant with a fungicide such as copper sulfate (1%) or mancozeb (2%). For best results, you should repeat spraying every 7-10 days until symptoms have disappeared completely.

To prevent this disease, make sure your area has proper soil drainage and fertilization, adequate air circulation around plants, and irrigate at midday when the sun is hottest to reduce the spread of the spores and avoid overwatering.

By following these steps, you can help to protect your tea plants from algal leaf spot disease, keeping them healthy for a long and productive life.

2. Brown Blight Disease

Brown blight disease is a fungus that affects tea plants and can cause significant damage or death to the plant if left untreated. The disease is caused by a fungal organism known as Alternaria alternata, which attacks the lower parts of the leaves and stems of tea plants. Infected tea leaves will have brown spots and eventually turn yellow and black. This discoloration of the foliage can lead to entire branches becoming affected, resulting in dieback and eventual death of the plant.

The best way to identify Brown blight disease is to look out for these symptoms: small, round lesions on the leaves; dark patches on their undersides; yellowing or wilting foliage; and dieback of branches. If any of these symptoms are present, you'll need to take immediate action to prevent the disease from spreading.

Maintaining good sanitation practices is the first step in preventing Brown blight disease. This means immediately removing any dead or diseased plants and leaves, disposing of them appropriately, and never transferring clippings or infected soil from one place to another. You should also always use clean gardening tools when pruning or harvesting your tea plants.

Monitor moisture levels in the area around your tea plants to ensure they are not too wet. Too much water can encourage fungal growth, so it is essential that the soil stays dry between watering. If your plants are in an area that is prone to high humidity, consider using a dehumidifier or other methods of reducing moisture in the air.

Finally, if you notice any signs of Brown blight disease in your tea plants, use a fungicide spray such as copper sulfate mixed with water according to the directions on the label. This should help to reduce and eliminate the fungal growth on your tea plants, keeping them healthy and productive for years to come.

Following these steps and practicing good sanitation when caring for your tea plants can prevent Brown blight disease from spreading and ensure that your plants remain happy and healthy. With diligent care and attention, you can enjoy delicious cups of tea made from your own tea plants for many years.

3. Gray Blight Disease

Gray blight is a common fungal disease of tea plants (Camellia sinensis) that can have devastating consequences for both commercial and backyard tea gardens. It is caused by the fungus Ramularia camelliae, which infects leaves and causes them to rot, leading to reduced yields.

Identifying gray blight is not always easy as its symptoms may be confused with other diseases or environmental issues such as nutrient deficiencies. Symptoms include yellowish-gray spots on the upper surface of leaves, gradually expanding until they cover the entire leaf surface. Depending on your location and season, these spots are typically olivaceous-brown in color but may also appear reddish-brown or black. Other symptoms include drying and curling of infected leaves, as well as wilting.

To prevent the spread of gray blight, understanding its life cycle and taking proactive measures to control it is key. The fungi overwinter in dead or decaying tissue, so removing infected plants from the garden and disposing of them properly can help reduce the chances of further spread. Cleaning tools regularly with alcohol or bleach will also help minimize the risk of infection. Pruning away affected branches can also be effective in reducing disease pressure on tea plants. Providing adequate drainage for your tea plants, avoiding over-watering, and applying mulch to help retain moisture levels in the soil will all help prevent disease. Rotating crops and using resistant varieties can also be helpful.

If you suspect gray blight, it is best to consult a professional who can diagnose the disease properly and recommend the appropriate treatment. Chemical fungicides may be necessary in some cases, so always follow instructions carefully when applying them. With proper prevention and control measures, it is possible to reduce the risk of gray blight in tea plants.

By following these steps, tea growers can help prevent the spread of gray blight and minimize its damaging effects on their other plants. With regular monitoring and diligent care, commercial tea gardens and backyard growers alike can enjoy healthy harvests for years to come.

4. Blister Blight

Blister blight is another fungal disease of tea plants that can cause significant crop losses if left unchecked. The disease, caused by the fungus Cercospora theae-sinensis, primarily affects the leaves of tea plants and can spread quickly from one plant to another. Symptoms of blister blight include small reddish-brown spots on both sides of the leaf blade, with white or yellow borders. Blisters may develop on the undersides of leaves, which can turn black as they enlarge. In severe cases, entire leaves may be destroyed, and defoliation can occur.

Tea growers should be aware of the signs and symptoms of blister blight to take swift action when needed. An accurate diagnosis is crucial for successful control methods. To identify the disease, look for reddish-brown spots on both sides of the leaf blade. The spots may have a white or yellow border around them. In severe cases, blisters will form on the undersides of leaves and turn black as they get bigger.

Practice good hygiene and crop rotation techniques to prevent blister blight from spreading. Start by removing any diseased leaves that are spotted and disposing of them away from other plants. Clean all your tools used in pruning or harvesting and sterilize them with a 10% bleach solution before moving to another plant. Additionally, rotate crops growing in the same area every two years to reduce the chance of recurrence.

Finally, use fungicides when needed to control the spread of the disease. To be effective, fungicides must be applied as soon as symptoms are spotted and repeated every two weeks or according to label instructions. This can help manage the fungus and reduce damage caused by blister blight.

By keeping an eye out for signs of this disease, you will be able to stop it before it spreads to all your plants. Following good hygiene practices, crop rotation techniques, and using fungicides when necessary, will help keep this fungal disease in check.

5. Horse Hair Blight

Horse hair blight disease is a fungal infection that is caused by the fungus Exobasidium vexans, which produces spores that spread through air or water. These spores can remain viable for up to four weeks in wet weather conditions.

When horsehair blight establishes itself in a tea plant, yellow spots appear on the underside of leaves, then progress to form white lesions on the leaf surface. As the disease spreads throughout the plant, its leaves become distorted and brittle, eventually turning brown and dying off. Infected plants are more prone to other diseases, such as black spots and scorch.

To prevent horse hair blight from spreading, it is essential to identify it in its early stages. Here are some steps to help you identify and prevent the disease:

1. Inspect your tea plants regularly for signs of yellow spots on the underside of leaves or white lesions on leaf surfaces.

2. If you find any infected plants, isolate them from other healthy plants and dispose of their foliage promptly.

3. Prune off dead branches to reduce the chances of further spread of the disease.

4. Water tea plants in dry conditions, as excessive moisture can lead to a greater risk of infection from horse hair blight spores.

5. Apply fungicides according to instructions to ensure that pathogens are destroyed before they can harm your tea crop.

6. Disinfect gardening tools before and after use to prevent the disease from spreading between plants.

7. Plant-resistant varieties of tea if available, as these have been developed to be more resilient against horse hair blight disease.

8. Rotate your plants and avoid planting tea plants in the same spot for several seasons to discourage the build-up of horse hair blight spores in the soil.

9. Remove any weeds or other debris from around your tea plants since these can act as a host for horse hair blight spores and increase the risk of infection.

10. Monitor environmental conditions such as temperature and humidity, as high levels of moisture create ideal conditions for fungal growth and spread.

11. If necessary, apply protective sprays containing copper sulfate during wet weather to prevent infection by horse hair blight.

12. Encourage natural predators, such as certain species of ladybugs and lacewings, which will feed on the horse hair blight spores before they can cause any further damage.

Following these steps can help protect your tea plants from horse hair blight disease and ensure a healthy crop for years to come. With proper monitoring and preventive measures in place, you can avoid the expense and hassle of dealing with this destructive fungal infection.

6. Twig Dieback

Twig dieback is a very serious and destructive disease that affects tea plants. A range of organisms, including fungi, bacteria, viruses, and nematodes causes it. The most common cause of twig dieback in tea plants is the fungus Phomopsis cantangensis. This disease can spread quickly throughout an entire crop if not managed properly.

Identifying the symptoms of twig dieback in tea plants is the first step to preventing its spread. The disease tends to appear as dark brown or black spots on the leaves, which then progress to branches that become stunted and misshapen with dead tips. As the infection progresses further, it will eventually kill whole branches or even entire plants in extreme cases.

In order to prevent twig dieback from spreading, keep the area around tea plants free of debris and weeds, remove any infected plant material as soon as possible, and avoid over-fertilizing or overwatering. Sanitation measures such as sterilizing pruning tools between uses can also help reduce the spread of the disease.

Finally, foliar sprays containing fungicides should be applied in early spring before any symptoms are visible on the plants. The most effective fungicides are based on copper, mancozeb, or azoxystrobin compounds, but these should always be used according to the manufacturer's instructions in order to minimize potential damage to the environment.

By following these steps, you can reduce the spread of twig dieback. With proper care and attention, healthy harvests of delicious tea leaves will surely follow.

How to Know if the Plant Is Incurable

The tea plant is a vulnerable species to diseases; however, incurable damage can be prevented when proper care is taken. Here are some tips on how to decide if the tea plant is sick or not and how to work out if it is incurable:

1. **Check for any signs of visible damage** – Look closely at the leaves of the plant, and if there are any discolored spots, wilting leaves, or other signs of damage that could indicate disease, then it's best to take action immediately by either removing the affected part or trying to treat the condition with appropriate measures such as pest control, fungicides, etc.

2. **Monitor soil nutrition** – Make sure that your soil has enough nutrients and moisture levels so that the tea plant is strong enough to resist any diseases.

3. **Examine its roots** – If you notice that the roots of your tea plant are discolored, mushy, or twisted, then it's a sign that

the plant may be suffering from an incurable disease and will need to be removed immediately.

4. **Keep watch for pests** – Pests such as aphids, mites, and scales can cause damage to the vegetation on your tea plants and make them more susceptible to diseases so it's significant to keep a close eye out for any signs of these little critters.

5. **Check for signs of decay** – As with any other living thing when a tea plant starts decaying due to age or disease, it will become discolored, wilted, and brittle. If you notice any of these signs, then it's best to take the necessary actions for treatment or removal as soon as possible so that the plant doesn't cause further damage to your garden.

By following these tips, you can determine whether the tea plant is incurable from diseases and take appropriate measures if required. Taking care of your tea plants will ensure they remain healthy and strong for years to come!

Strategies to Cure Tea Plants

1. **Biological Control:** Biological control is a process of introducing a natural enemy, such as an insect or fungus, to combat the disease-causing fungi or bacteria on plants. This method can be most effective when used in conjunction with cultivation that promotes healthy plant growth and reduces the spread of disease. For example, if a soil-borne pathogen is attacking crops, planting them in well-drained soil with

improved air and water movement around the roots can help reduce the incidence of disease. Additionally, certain beneficial species of fungi are able to out-compete the pathogens responsible for diseases like damping off, root rots, and blight; this helps to rid plants of their harmful effects and increases crop production.

2. **Chemical Control**: Chemical control involves using fungicides or bactericides to prevent or treat certain plant diseases. These chemicals are generally applied as a spray onto the foliage of infected plants to control and reduce the spread of disease-causing organisms. While chemical control may be an effective method for controlling plant diseases in some cases, it should be used judiciously since many chemicals are toxic to the targeted organism and other beneficial organisms like insects and bees that assist in pollination. Additionally, overuse can lead to increased resistance among pathogens, making them more difficult to treat in future instances.

3. **Crop Rotation:** Crop rotation involves moving plants around your space each year so that different nutrient needs are met by each crop variety, as well as helping to limit pest and disease problems from reoccurring. For example, in commercial enterprises, growing a variety of peas one season, followed by wheat, then corn, then soybeans over subsequent years help break up pest cycles between those individual crops while providing new levels of nutrients

needed for each type's healthy growth cycle throughout as well as reducing potential disease pressure.

4. **Pruning:** Pruning is another component for combating various plant diseases by removing diseased branches from trees or shrubs, thereby eliminating possible pathways for spores from infested areas from spreading further.

5. **Sanitation Practices:** Sanitation practices involve keeping tools free from contaminants such as spores — and also making sure you clean your hands before touching plants — which can reduce the introduction and spread of potentially dangerous microbes among plants during cultivation processes (i.e., weeding). By following these simple steps, you can help keep your garden free from unnecessary infections caused by human mishandling leading to potentially devastating blight outbreaks within your gardens.

How to Deal with Diseased Tea Plants

The most crucial step in dealing with a damaged tea plant is to remove it without spreading the illness to other plants. It is necessary to take certain precautions when removing an infected tea plant so as not to cause further damage and infection.

The first step is to identify the source of the disease and isolate it from the others. If the plant shows signs of wilting or discoloration, these are indicators that something may be wrong and should be closely monitored for potential signs of disease. Once identified, the affected plant must be removed promptly to prevent further contamination of healthy plants.

Removing a diseased tea plant correctly will reduce the spreading of any diseases. The best way to do it is by hand. This means carefully cutting away any infected parts of the plant and disposing of them in a sealed bag or container.

Another option is to use tools such as pruners or shears to cut away any diseased parts of the plant. These tools must be disinfected before and after use so as not to spread any disease further. It is also crucial that all removed material is disposed of in a safe manner, either by burning or burying it away from other plants.

In some cases, chemical treatments may need to be used to eradicate a disease from an entire tea plantation or garden. Always exercise caution when using chemicals, as they can be highly toxic and should never be used near edible crops or humans.

By following proper precautions, diseased tea plants can be removed safely and efficiently, and you will curtail the spread of disease. Taking the time to identify, isolate, and remove any infected plants is a simple but vital step that every tea gardener should take in order to ensure the health of their entire crop.

Chapter 7

Creating Tea Blends

Tea blends are made from a range of ingredients like essential oils, fruits, blossoms, herbs, or other types of teas, unlike pure tea, which contains only one type of plant. Blended teas usually have a stronger taste because they include either artificial or natural flavors. Although you can blend any tea, black tea is the most common and popular type.

The quality and flavor of tea blends differ from one company to another. Various synthetic aromatics, additives, and artificial flavors are usually added to tea blends to strengthen and improve their scent and taste. Companies also use synthetic dyes, which aren't always safe. These artificial ingredients are usually added to cheap blends to cover their low quality. For instance, you can buy jasmine tea with a nice fragrance, but when you brew it, it loses its aroma, and the taste turns bitter. Creating your own tea blends at home is the better and safer option. You will have control over the ingredients and only focus on natural ones instead of less healthy additives.

Although blending tea is a simple process, it's also very unique. Each blend must have a base that can be either dried herbs or pure tea. Any type of pure tea can be incorporated into the blends, like green or black tea, which are more common, or puerh, oolong, or white tea as well. On the other hand, blending herbal tea uses various types of herbs like peppermint, rooibos, tulsi, and chamomile. These herbs don't contain any caffeine since they don't come from a tea plant.

Blending tea doesn't only enhance the quality, but you can also create blends that promote relaxation and boost your immunity.

Best Flavors to Blend Together

Some blends can work together, while others don't. For instance, it isn't recommended to mix black and green tea together because black tea has a powerful flavor, and this blend can result in an overpowering taste. Black tea works better with fruit pieces and spices. Green tea has a softer flavor, so it's usually blended with herbs, the same with white tea. If you mix black and green tea, you will not taste a blend of any other ingredient but mainly a black tea flavor with a small hint of green tea.

Beginners can be overwhelmed by the many flavors and ingredients required to create a good tea blend. Before you start blending, try a few tea mixes to discover your favorite flavors. Check local tea stores, where you will find various blends to try. There are also tea experts who can give you tips on which ingredients and teas work together.

Flavors That Work Together

- Mixing bold and spicy flavors can create a strong tea blend with a powerful taste. Black tea and spices are some of the most popular tea blends. If you don't like bitter flavors, you can soften the taste by adding sweet or sugary ingredients like vanilla while still enjoying the spices and the bold flavor of black tea.

- Bold flavors also work with sweet ones. Mixing black tea with chocolate or vanilla will create a layered, rich, and deep taste.

- For the ultimate sugary flavor, try sweet and fruity ingredients that will feel more like a dessert than a regular cup of tea. It's perfect for people with a sweet tooth.

Ingredients to Blend with Black Tea

- Use black tea as a base, then add a hint of cardamom, lemongrass, and ginger. If you enjoy Thai tea, you will love this blend. Brew this blend in hot milk instead of water.

- Mix black tea with cinnamon, almond powder, and pieces of dehydrated apples.

- Blend cloves, cinnamon, and orange peel with black tea. This blend will have earthy notes with a hot cinnamon spice flavor and a hint of clover. The orange will serve as a secondary flavor.

- For this blend, mix many types of black tea like Darjeeling, Assam, and Ceylon with a small number of coffee beans. This is the perfect cup of tea to drink in the morning since it is very strong.

- Mix black tea with vanilla beans and peppermint. If you want to prepare a festive tea, add a small amount of candy cane to the mix.

Ingredients to Blend with Herbal Tea

- Begin with chamomile as the base and mix rose petals with rose buds and lavender. This blend can aid in relaxation and promote better sleep.

- Mix peppermint with fennel and chamomile. This blend can relieve stomach aches.

- Use chamomile as a base, then add orange peels, rose buds, and cornflowers. This blend has a citrus flavor and is very light. You can drink it anytime during the day or when you are in need of a decaffeinated cup of tea.

- Mix licorice roots with turmeric and infuse hot water and add ginger to the mix. Then add orange peels and lemongrass. While brewing, add honey for a sweet flavor.

Ingredients to Blend with Green Tea

- Mix green tea with mint. This simple blend is perfect for beginners who don't want to overwhelm their palette. Bitter green tea and fresh mint make the perfect tea blend.

- Mix green tea with cloves, cinnamon, orange peel, and pieces of dehydrated apples. This blend's flavor tastes like candied apples.

- Mix green tea with rooibos tea and elderberry, rose hips, cinnamon, hibiscus, and canella. You will get a strong green tea flavor with a hint of tartness,

- Mix green tea with sweet rhubarb, raspberry, and apple, then add a small amount of vanilla. This blend will have a citrus flavor.

- Mix green tea with strawberry, Curcuma, rose, cherry, and goji berry. For a spicier flavor, add turmeric to the mix.

- Mix green tea with dried and frozen raspberry and lemon peel. This blend is both tasty and healthy.

The Benefits of Tea Blending

Learning any new skill can be intimidating at first. However, tea blending is fun and easy. It is a practical skill that will allow you to contribute to the world as you prepare nutritional blends to help others.

Creativity

Blending tea is an interesting hobby that allows you to be creative. You don't only mix ingredients to prepare tea for various ailments and benefit from their nutrients, but as you familiarize yourself with the process, you can also start creating your own recipes. Similar to painting or learning a musical instrument, blending tea is an artistic skill. Everyone needs a creative outlet to take a break from their hectic everyday life. If you can't find a relaxing hobby, try tea blending.

Connects You with Nature

Connecting with nature is good for your physical and mental health. You don't need to go camping or walk in a forest to establish this connection. Many tea enthusiasts say that this hobby makes them feel close to nature since they work with natural ingredients like herbs or plants. Herbs contain many health benefits that you can learn about while blending tea. Discovering what each herb has to offer will make you more appreciative of nature and strengthen your bond with it. You will realize that nature is sufficient since it provides you with everything you need, including remedies for various ailments.

Empowering

Blending tea will empower you as you learn about the healing properties of the different blends you can create. Experimenting with various ingredients will teach you about your body as you find out what flavors and fragrances you prefer and which ones will trigger a negative response from you. Preparing blends with healing properties for your family and friends can make you feel powerful as you help others and make a difference in the world. Many people have also become entrepreneurs and built successful businesses from blending tea.

Anyone Can Do It

Anyone can blend tea; you don't have to be an herbalist to practice this activity. Research various herbs, learn about their benefits, understand what your body needs, and experiment with different blends.

The Benefits of Tea Blends

Tea blends don't only produce a tasty and unique flavor, but they also have many health benefits. The ingredients in tea blends can provide you with various nutrients.

Black and Oolong Tea Blends

Black and oolong tea blends contain polyphenols which reduce the signs of aging.

Green Tea Blends

Green tea blends have many health benefits. They rejuvenate the skin and boost your attention span. Green tea also has anti-carcinogenic properties; it can reduce the risk of prostate cancer, breast cancer, and other types of cancers as well. It also has anti-inflammatory properties, which can protect the blood vessels, lower blood pressure, and reduce the risk of cardiovascular disease.

Sencha Green Tea Blends

Who said children can't drink tea? Sencha green tea is safe for children since it doesn't contain caffeine, is made with natural products, and can make them feel refreshed. Since children usually run and play all the time, they sweat more than adults. Drinking sencha green tea blends can make up for the salt they lose while sweating. Children can drink this tea blend when they have a cold, as it can speed up their recovery.

Hibiscus Tea Blends

Hibiscus tea blends aren't your typical teas. They can make you feel refreshed and quench your thirst. This blend can also reduce cellulite in the body, aid in digestion, and improve the kidneys' health. Regular consumption of hibiscus tea can lower your blood pressure.

White Tea Blends

White tea blends can aid in weight loss as white tea can break down fat cells and prevent the growth of new ones.

Chamomile Tea Blends

Chamomile tea blends have sedative properties that can promote relaxation, aid in sleeping, and reduce stress and anxiety.

Ginger Tea Blends

Ginger tea blends can be an effective remedy for various respiratory issues like asthma and chest congestion. The blend can open up and soothe the airways.

Rooibos Tea Blends

Rooibos tea blends contain anti-inflammatory properties that can soothe stomach aches and relax muscles.

Blending your own tea is also much healthier than store-bought tea. You can add the flavors you like and avoid artificial ingredients that can harm your health.

Tips and Tricks for Blending Tea

- Don't be afraid to experiment with different ingredients. Different fruits and herbs can be added to your blends, enhancing the tea's flavor and aroma. Whether it's lemon, apples, or strawberries, try everything, and you will be surprised by the results.

- For tea blending to work, make sure that the taste remains consistent yet subtly reflects the flavor of each ingredient.

- Adding blossoms or pieces of fruit to your tea blends will enhance the tea's quality and aroma; however, they will not improve the taste. For a better flavor, add flowers or fruits with the leaves and leave them to settle for some time to give the scent a chance to infuse with the tea leaves.

- There are no rules to tea blending. You can create your own recipes and list of ingredients depending on your mood and needs. Listen to your body, connect with your intuition, and start creating. The end results of each recipe you prepare will be a surprise to your taste buds.

- You can add natural flavors to your ingredients and mix them with fruits or petals to improve the tea's fragrance, flavor, and quality.

- Start small with only two ingredients and go up from there. Don't overwhelm yourself while you are still in the learning process; take your time, and eventually, you will be ready for the more complex blends.

- Dehydrated ingredients are your best option when blending tea. It is easier to brew dry ingredients, and their flavor is very powerful.

- Tea should always be the main ingredient in all your blends. About two-thirds of every blend needs to be tea. For light tea, use low-concentrated and soft ingredients. Avoid strong herbs that can intensify the flavor and aroma of your blend. Chamomile and lavender can create a balanced experience, while herbs like ginger and cardamom can produce a strong taste.

- Familiarizing yourself with many tea flavors will make the blending process much easier. This can take you years since there are many types of teas, herbs, fruits, aromas, etc. Start by learning about the fragrances and flavors of the flowers in your gardens and the herbs and spices in your kitchen.

- Protect your tea from "de-blending" by using ingredients that have the same size and density. Tea experts advise against blending ingredients that differ in size as the heavy parts will fall at the bottom and lessen the tea and flavor's quality.

- Crush spices before adding them to your tea blend. If you are going to use dried fruits, cut them into small pieces, all similar in size. When using flowers, you will need either the buds or petals.

- Taste each ingredient you are going to use before incorporating it into your blend to determine if it is going to work with the tea blend you are preparing or not.

- Prepare your equipment before you start — airtight containers, measuring spoons, flavoring, base tea, measuring glass, and dried fruits, herbs, or spices (if you have a dehydrator, you can dry them yourself or use fresh ingredients instead).

- Learn about the different terms in tea blending. For instance, the tea base is the foundation of your blend, and it determines the other ingredients you will use since they must complement it.

- Create different blends depending on the season. Floral, fruity, and sweet blends are appropriate for spring and summer, while nutty, fire, and spicy blends are perfect for fall and winter.

- Store your blended tea in an airtight container in a cool, dark, and dry space.

Tea Blending Is an Art

Tea blending is an art. Similar to painting or writing, this skill requires creativity and imagination. By observing the tea blending process, you will notice that you create something powerful out of small pieces. Just like art, you have the freedom to imagine and create. There are no recipes, restrictions, or rules to follow. You choose the ingredients that you want. The end result isn't just a cup of tea but a form of self-expression and a part of who you are.

The purpose of each ingredient is to balance the favor. You should taste the flavors of every herb, spice, and fruit while also experiencing the taste of the whole blend. Just as an artist focuses on each color they use and its impact on a painting, tea blending requires you to focus on each ingredient to determine if it will improve, empower, soften, or have no impact on the flavor.

On the surface, blending tea and fusing flavors sound simple. This process isn't a scientific experiment where you have numbers and equations to follow. It is an art, and you can let your imagination run as far as it can go. This can make blending tea more complex, following a recipe or a list of rules to make the process easier as there is no room for error. However, when you are creating something without a guide, you always expect perfection, like a painting; you can ruin it by using one wrong color.

Blending tea is quite similar to making perfumes. You start with a base note that acts as a strong foundation and then add all the other ingredients that will activate the flavor and aroma. For instance, if you want to create a blend to promote relaxation, your base note can be chamomile which is known for reducing stress and keeping you calm, balance the flavor with rose petals, and add mint to contrast with the earthy flavor of chamomile.

Common Tea Blending Methods

Mini Tea Blends

Mini blending is when you blend just one ingredient with your tea or herb. By using this method, you can learn how one ingredient can impact your tea flavor. You can keep changing this one ingredient and experiment with different flavors. You already have the tea or herb acting as the base of the blend, and you can use a new ingredient each time until you find a flavor you like.

Mixing Tea Blends

If you are reluctant about experimenting with ingredients right away and creating your own tea blends, try mixing different tea blends together to create a new one. Start simple with just two blends that share the same base, whether herb or tea. Mix them together in a bowl, then make a cup of tea to try the new flavor you created. If the flavors don't complement each other or one flavor overpowers the rest, change the ratio, or try different blends altogether.

Expand Your Tea Blends

This requires you to reach a more advanced level of tea blending. Use the mini tea blends method but expand on it.

- Choose a base ingredient, whether herb or tea

- Next, add a complementary ingredient that enhances the first one

- Add one last ingredient to enhance the flavor

Work with a 3:2:1 ratio, with the base ingredient acting as the main one. If the flavor is lacking, choose one or more ingredients of your choice to improve the tea's quality and taste.

Blending tea is a simple and creative activity that can enhance your creativity. You aren't governed by a specific recipe, so you can experiment with as many different ingredients as you like. Have a purpose for your tea blend. Decide whether you are making a blend to enjoy a delicious cup of tea or for nutritional purposes so you can determine which ingredients to use. Remember to always start small. Whether you are mixing ingredients or tea blends, don't overwhelm yourself. As you gain more experience and learn about your favorite flavors, you can expand.

Tea blending doesn't only connect you with nature but with the people in your life as well. It can be a group activity where you use your imaginative skills with your loved ones and create something special.

Let your imagination run wild and get creative with various tea blend flavors.

Chapter 8

Tea Brewing Methods

Tea brewing is the process of making tea where you steep tea bags or tea leaves in water and then boil them to make a cup of tea. Although this is the most common method for brewing tea, there are different ways to make a hot or cold cup of tea. This chapter will cover several easy tea-brewing methods so you can discover new brewing methods for a good cup of tea.

Cold Brewing

Cold brewing is the best method to make iced tea. It is a process where you steep tea in water and leave it in the refrigerator for a few hours. Although it is a simple process, it takes the tea a long time to reach the right temperature in the fridge, so preparing it a day in advance if you have guests coming over or a party is recommended.

Some people think that cold brewing is simply adding ice to hot brewed tea. Although this can work if you are in a hurry, it won't have the same taste or quality as cold brewing. Cold brewing and hot brewing aren't the same. Each method is used for preparing a different type of tea. The tea leaves in cold brewing usually take their time to infuse, which creates compounds different from that of hot brewing. The long process of cold brewing is necessary for the tea to produce complex and rich aromas and flavors. It also prevents the bitter flavor notes that are usually released during hot brewing.

Cold brewing works with any type of tea. It is also the perfect method for people who don't like caffeinated beverages since it drastically reduces caffeine. The end result is a calming, refreshing, and smooth cup of iced tea.

This brewing method is very safe. Since you store the tea infusion in the fridge, it is protected against heat and bacteria growth that can impact its flavor and quality. However, some ingredients require rinsing with hot water before brewing, like flowers, herbs, puerh, and white tea, to kill the bacteria. The healthy antioxidants in the tea also remain intact even though it is kept in the fridge for several hours.

Making cold brewed tea is very simple, and it doesn't require tools or many ingredients. You will need a brewing vessel, water, filter, and tea leaves (or tea bags). For this process to work, use the correct tools. Using high-quality and flavored tea. Pay attention to the brewing vessel as well. Make sure to clean, sterilize it, and check for cracks before using it. You can use a large pitcher, a plastic container, a glass jar, or a bottle. Make sure that whatever you use has a lid to protect the tea from the taste and scent of other food in the fridge.

Iced tea is perfect for spring and summer, and it gives you the freedom to experiment with different flavors and ingredients. You can also mix the tea with your favorite summer cocktail. Cold brewing produces sweeter tea than its counterpart, so it doesn't require any artificial sweeteners.

How to Cold Brew Tea

Tools:

- Brewing vessel

- Filter pouch

Ingredients:

- 1 teaspoon of loose tea leaves (or one tea bag) of your favorite tea for 1 cup of water. If you are making a batch, use 4 to 5 teaspoons of tea leaves or 3 to 5 tea bags for every quart

- Lemon slices, cucumber slices, or fresh mint leaves (optional)

Instructions:

1. Place the tea leaves or tea bags in the brewing pitcher (to get a strong flavor, cut off the tea bag corners and pour its content into the pitcher).

2. Add cool or room-temperature water to the tea and cover the pitcher with a lid.

3. Leave the tea in the fridge for 2 to 8 hours (ideally, let it brew overnight).

4. When it is ready, take the pitcher out of the fridge and pour the tea using a filter (if you are using tea bags, just pull them out).

5. Top the tea with slices of lemons, cucumbers, or mint leaves for extra flavor.

Tips

- For herbal, oolong, or black tea, let it steep for eight to twelve hours.

- For green and white tea, let it steep for six to eight hours.

- Add ice for a more refreshing beverage and to keep it cooler for a longer period of time.

- Check the brewing time for each type of tea first. Some teas can turn bitter if they aren't brewed properly.

- For beginners, choose teas that are easy to brew, like herbal, oolong, and black tea.

- You can make a batch of cold-brewed tea, store it in the fridge, and drink it for several days.

- Don't store cold brewed tea for over four days.

- If you don't want to use a filter or change pitchers, cold brew the tea in a cold-brew tea maker.

- Although you can use plastic containers, glass containers are preferable since they won't stain or impact the tea's odor.

Hot Brewing

Hot tea brewing is the more common method, where you make a cup of tea by boiling water and pouring it over the tea leaves. Consuming hot brewed tea reduces the risk of type 2 diabetes, heart disease, and Alzheimer's. It also aids in digestion, improves your mood, reduces stress, and boosts immunity.

Most people assume that you can make tea by heating a cup of water in the microwave. However, microwave temperatures are hot and hard, which can be too harsh on the soft tea leaves. With hot tea brewing, you pour the water slowly over the loose tea-leaf and leave them to release their rich flavors.

Proper hot tea brewing will give you high-quality tea with a better flavor. Making a cup of tea may seem simple enough, but there are a few mistakes that people usually make, and they end up with a weak taste. One of the most common brewing mistakes is using tap water. Remember that water is a main ingredient in tea brewing. Spring and filtered water will enhance the tea's flavor and your overall experience.

Don't add many ingredients to your cup of tea before tasting the flavor first. Adding milk is fine, but adding cream or lemons can impact the flavor. Ingredients are fine for tea bags, but loose-leaf tea contains strong flavors that don't require extra ingredients.

Infusing tea leaves three or four times will give you a chance to experience a different taste each time. However, the flavor and caffeine won't be as strong, but the exciting tea experience multiple infusions provide you is worth it. For instance, after the first infusion, a cup of tea can have an intense flavor, but after a couple of infusions, you can notice a softer or floral taste.

There are various ways you can make hot brew tea. You can make a cup of tea with a kettle or without one. The third method is a traditional Chinese method called "gaiwan," which is more complex but provides an accurate and delicious tea experience.

Method #1: Hot Brewing with a Kettle

Tools:

- Kettle

- Teapot

- Filter

Ingredients:

- 1 tablespoon of loose black tea-leaf

- 3 cups of filtered water (you will need 2 cups of water to make the tea. The extra cup is for warming the teapot)

Instructions:

1. Set the temperature on your electric kettle to 208°F. Pour the three cups of water into the kettle and leave them to boil.

2. Pour about a cup of hot water into the teapot. Swirl it around for a few seconds or until it warms up. Throw away the water afterward.

3. Add the tea to the teapot, then pour the hot water from the kettle over the tea.

4. Place the lid over the teapot and leave the tea to steep for five minutes.

5. Pour the tea into cups using a filter to remove the tea solids.

Method #2: Hot Brewing without a Kettle

Tools:

- Small saucepan

- Teapot

Ingredients:

- 1 tablespoon of tea leaves or 1 tea bag

- 1 cup of filtered water

Instructions:

1. Get a small saucepan and wash it thoroughly.

2. Pour the filtered water into the saucepan.

3. Leave it to boil on the stove.

4. Add the tea leaves to the teapot, then pour the hot water.

5. Leave it to steep for two to five minutes.

6. Remove the tea bag or the tea solid using a filter.

Method #3: Hot Brewing Chinese Gaiwan

Gaiwan is a Chinese word that means "lidded bowl" or "lidded cup." This method works with any type of tea, especially ones with delicate flavors like white and green tea. It is one of the oldest tea-brewing methods in the world, as Chinese people have been using it for centuries. For this process to work, you will only need a gaiwan which consists of a saucer, lid, and bowl. It acts as both a teapot and a teacup, so you can brew and drink the tea from it.

Tools:

*   Gaiwan

Ingredients:

*   Tea leaves (enough for one-third of a gaiwan)

*   Water

Instructions:

1. Wash the gaiwan with hot water and rinse thoroughly to clean it from any residue or dust. The hot water should also warm up the gaiwan before you add the tea leaves.

2. Rinse the tea leaves to open them up and release their fragrance. Savor the tea's aroma before you start brewing to prepare your taste buds for the tea flavor.

3. Add the tea leaves to the gaiwan (experiment with the quantity and keep adjusting to your taste).

4. Boil water in a kettle or saucepan, then pour the hot water into the gaiwan to cover the tea leaves, then discard the water right away.

5. Remove the gaiwan's lid and enjoy the tea fragrance for a while (the tea's aroma experience is as significant as the flavor).

6. Next, boil more water and pour it into the gaiwan and leave the tea to steep for a while.

7. Drink the tea right from the gaiwan by holding the saucer in your right palm. Tilt the lid away with your left hand and sip. If you don't want to drink the tea from the gaiwan, pour it into cups.

N.B.

- Leave black and oolong tea to steep from 45 seconds to 1 minute with the lid on.

- Leave green tea to steep for 30 to 45 seconds with the lid off.

Method #4: Ice Tea

Although cold brewing is the best method for iced tea, you can experiment with hot brewing as well.

Tools:

- A small saucepan

- Shaker

Ingredients:

- Oolong, rooibos, or black tea leaves

- Water

- Sweetener

Instructions:

1. Wash a small saucepan and pour a cup of water into it.

2. Leave it to boil on the stove, then add the tea leaves (experiment with the quantity until you find a flavor you like).

3. Leave the tea to simmer over a low fire for five minutes.

4. Fill a shaker with ice and then pour the tea through a filter.

5. Add sweetener if you prefer, then close the shaker and shake it.

6. Pour the iced tea into a glass, and add lemon slices if you like.

Tips

- Clean your cups, kettle, and teapot before brewing.

- With tea bags, avoid overboiling the water as it reduces the oxygen and impacts the taste, so pour the water the moment it boils.

- For a six-ounce cup, use either one teaspoon of tea leaves or one tea bag.

- The flavor depends on the steeping time. If you don't give the tea the right steeping time, it will have a weak aroma and taste. Don't assume that the tea is brewed just because it changes color. Developing flavor takes longer.

- Each tea type has its own brewing time, so make sure you leave the tea to steep according to its recommended time.

- Black, chai, and iced tea take about 3-5 minutes to brew, while green tea takes 2 minutes, white tea takes about 1 to 2 minutes, it takes herbal and red 3 to 4 minutes, and it takes oolong 2 to 3 minutes.

- Never use the microwave to boil water, as it can impact the taste.

- Reduce the brewing time if you want a weaker taste and increase it if you want a strong flavor.

- Each type of tea requires a different boiling degree. Green, oolong, and white tea require cool water, so the heating temperature should be between 158°F to 185°F. Dark tea, like herbal and black teas, requires a higher temperature of about 200°F.

- Leaving the tea for a couple of minutes to cool down is vital as it will give the tea a chance to release subtle flavors.

- Warm the teapot with hot water before using it.

- Similar to tea blending, brewing also invites a lot of creativity. The quantity of tea leaves mainly depends on your taste. Keep adjusting the quantity until you reach the desired taste. The same applies to ingredients; you can experiment with different ones and create new flavors.

- Avoid metal and plastic gaiwans since they can impact the flavor of the tea. Choose glass or glazed ceramic material.

- Unlike cold-brewed tea, hot-brewed tea can't be stored and should be consumed a few minutes after preparation.

Brewing Herbal Tea

Herbal tea is either brewed as a decoction or infusion. With decoction, the herbs are simmered and produce a much stronger and more concentrated flavor, while the infusion draws out the aroma and vitamins from the plants.

Herbal Decoction

Tools:

- Saucepan

- Filter

Ingredients:

- 1 tablespoon of your favorite organic herbs (you can use one type of herb or more)

- 8 ounces of water

Instructions:

1. Place the herbs in a small saucepan and pour the water over them.

2. Cover the saucepan with a lid and leave it to simmer for 10 to 12 minutes.

3. Pour the tea into a cup using a filter, leave it to cool down, and then drink.

Herbal Infusions

Tools:

- Tea filter

- Cup

Ingredients:

- 1 tablespoon of your favorite organic herbs

- 8 ounces of water

Instructions:

1. Heat the water to 180-212°F.

2. Put the herbs in a cup using a tea filter or a tea infuser.

3. Pour the hot water over the herbs and leave them for 3 to 5 minutes to steep.

4. Remove the infuser and drink your tea.

Chai Decoction

Chai is one of the oldest teas in the world, and it also acts as an herbal remedy. It relieves pain, improves blood circulation, and aids in digestion. This tea originated in India, and it is made from different spices. It doesn't contain any tea leaves. Chai can be brewed as an infusion or decoction.

Tools:

- Saucepan

- Filter

- Cup

Ingredients:

- 1 tablespoon of your favorite organic chai blend

- 4 ounces of organic milk (you can use water or any other milk substitute)

- 8 ounces of water

- 2 to 3 teaspoons of your favorite organic sweetener

Instructions:

1. Put the chai tea blend in a small saucepan.

2. Pour the water and milk into the saucepan.

3. Leave them to simmer for about ten minutes.

4. Next, pour the chai into a cup through a filter

5. Add in the sweetener

Chai Infusion

Ingredients:

- 1 tablespoon of your favorite organic chai blend

- 8 ounces of water

Instructions:

1. Put the herbs in a tea filter or tea infuser.

2. Pour hot water over the herbs and let them steep for 3 to 5 minutes.

3. Take out the infuser and drink the tea.

Brewing Fresh Plants

Seeing that blending tea is an art, get creative with the different plants while brewing to make a delicious cup of tea. You can use one type of plant but if you want a strong taste, brew various types of plants together.

Tools:

- Saucepan

- Teapot

- Filter

Ingredients:

- 2 to 3 tablespoons of fresh plants (seeds, flowers, or herbs)

- Water

- Honey (or sugar or a sugar substitute)

Instructions:

1. Rinse the plants thoroughly.

2. Place water in a small saucepan and leave it to boil.

3. Put the plants in a teapot, then pour the hot water.

4. Leave them to steep for five minutes or until the water changes color.

5. Remove the plants from the tea using a filter, then add the honey.

French Press Brewing

People usually use the French Press method to brew their coffee, but it is also a popular brewing method among tea enthusiasts. French Press will provide you with delicious tea rich in flavor.

Tools:

- French Press
- Small saucepan

Ingredients:

- ¼ cup of tea leaves (for a four-cup press)
- Water
- Cream or sugar (optional)

Instructions:

1. Wash your French Press thoroughly to remove any coffee residue.

2. Add water to a small saucepan and leave it to boil.

3. Put the tea leaves in the French Press.

4. Pour the hot water over the tea leaves.

5. Leave them to steep for 1 to 2 minutes.

6. Press on the French Press plunger to filter the tea leaves from the tea.

7. Pour all the tea into cups. Make sure there isn't any liquid left so you can brew the tea leaves again.

8. Sweeten the tea with cream or sugar.

Brewing tea is easy. Although there are certain rules and guidelines that you should follow, there is always room for creativity, whether with the tea blends or quantities. Make sure to pay attention to the brewing time of each type of tea. Leaving the tea to brew for longer than it should results in a bitter flavor, while leaving it for a short time can weaken the taste.

You can use high-quality tea and follow the instructions, yet the tea's flavor can feel lacking. In this case, you should consider switching to filter water. Filter water will provide you with a clear and strong taste. The material of the pitchers and teapots is of equal significance as well. Stick to glass as it is the safest option and will not impact the tea's flavor.

If you are a coffee drinker and are new to the world of tea brewing, consider trying the French Press method. It will be easy and familiar, and you can brew the tea leaves more than once.

Now that you have become familiar with various tea brewing methods, you are ready to make the perfect cup of tea.

Chapter 9

Tea Blends for Anxiety

Do you suffer from anxiety due to worries, tension, a sudden traumatic event, or stress, and would you want to live a happy, healthy life? Then learn to de-stress and relax your mind regularly with the power of tea blends.

You may find making tea from different plants challenging due to tight schedules and a lack of ingredients, but storing herbs in dried form can help you relax in the shortest amount of time. These tea blends can help you deal with stress and mild anxiety.

Constant anxiety that you cannot control can affect you physically and externally. This chapter will focus on the various tea blends used to combat anxiety.

Herbal teas are healthy and inexpensive to produce. You can also grow your favorite herbs in your garden and preserve them in your kitchen throughout the year.

Hot drinks are the most practical way to feel comfortable, at ease, and warm. Many have become part of a nightly ritual of winding down to promote relaxation, aid sleep, and reduce stress.

If you are allergic to certain herbs, you should be aware of the ingredient and make sure it's not in the tea you drink to help you sleep. Some tea blends keep you awake rather than sleepy, so you should note the core component of the tea blend to achieve the desired result.

Avoid herbal tea containing caffeine if you want to relax and reduce anxiety. Because teas made from herbs have many healthy components that can help you feel calmer, a special tea selection can help reduce stress and anxiety.

Although it is difficult to predict when anxiety will strike, you will be prepared if you grow your favorite herbs in your garden, dry and store them in your pantry.

Dried herbs, such as dried ginger root, can be ground. Before storing them in an airtight, transparent container, ensure they are completely dry.

Valerian root, chamomile, lemon balm, lavender, and other herbs create pure, home-brewed tea blends with different flavors. Don't worry if you are not a perfect tea blender; instead, focus on blending flavors that will help you manage your anxiety and satisfy your taste buds.

You should try different flavors until you find one that works best for you because different flavors suit different people.

For ways to relax a tense or anxious nervous system, herbal medicines have been useful for centuries. You can use many different herbs to create special relaxing and de-stressing teas using nettle leaf, Gotu kola, kava, ashwagandha tea, ginger, lemon balm, lemongrass, passionflower, peppermint, valerian root, holy basil, rose tea, lavender, and chamomile.

Brew any of the tea blends discussed below for the best tea combinations for stress and anxiety:

Chamomile and Lavender Tea

A delicate garden flower known as chamomile has long been lauded for its anti-stress properties. Its apigenin content can help with relaxation, insomnia, inflammation, and menstrual pain.

Chamomile contains sedative properties and has been used successfully in treating anxiety disorders. The taste of chamomile by itself is bland and could use some zing! Lavender is one of the most relaxing herbs. When you combine lavender and chamomile flowers, you get a caffeine-free stress-relieving tea.

This tea blend can be enjoyed whenever you want and is best served lukewarm. Taking lavender tea on its own is beneficial but not as effective when mixed with chamomile tea. This tea blend is regarded as the most potent of all herbal remedies.

Flavor note: Chamomile will excite your taste buds with a handful of sweetness and lavender's minty strong floral. This duo is a wonderful combination.

Ingredients:

- One teaspoon of dried chamomile or a tablespoon of fresh chamomile.

- A dash or half teaspoon of organic lavender.

- A cup of boiled water.

Instructions:

In a clean pot, combine all the ingredients, add the boiled water, and steep for 20 minutes before straining. Sweeten to taste and serve (sweetener can be stevia or honey).

Peppermint and Valerian Root

There is no better way to unwind before bedtime than with a cup of this tea blend. The aroma will relax you and relieve any nervousness or anxiety you may have felt throughout the day.

Menthol, a powerful component found in peppermint, has been used for centuries to increase relaxation, treat constipation, and improve digestive issues. It also helps relieve chronic pain and migraines. Peppermint tea relieves headaches while also being delicious.

A blend of valerian root and peppermint leaves aid sleep naturally. Valerian tea is known for its stress-relieving properties, making it a popular natural remedy for headaches, heart palpitations, and insomnia. Aside from these advantages, valerian root also effectively treats chronic pain symptoms, sleep disorders, and anxiety.

Valerian root has been used as an effective herbal remedy for centuries. When taken as a tea, valerian root regulates GABA levels in the brain, promoting nerve impulse regulation and reducing anxiety and stress while lowering blood pressure.

Valerian tea naturally helps you maintain focus and think clearly. As a standalone herbal tea, it has a calming effect in stressful situations; however, when combined with peppermint, the effectiveness is increased.

Flavor note: Peppermint gives off a mint flavor and taste that soothes the mouth and throat. Valerian root has a mild flavor that is light in the mouth. You can enjoy this blend without sweetener if you don't like sweetened tea.

Ingredients:

- A teaspoon of dried valerian root.

- Two tablespoons of fresh peppermint leaves or a tablespoon of dried leaves.

- A cup of boiled water.

Instructions:

Fill a clean pot or cup halfway with boiling water, then add the dried valerian root and peppermint leaves. Allow at least 5 minutes for the herbs to infuse before straining. Add your preferred sweetener.

Chamomile, Lemongrass, and Passionflower

Floral flavors pair well with various herbs, and passionflower is one of those floral flavors. Passionflower complements lemongrass and chamomile well. It is a well-known tropical flower for relieving anxiety and insomnia.

You might be wondering why lemongrass. This is because it is high in antioxidants, which help the body fight free radicals. In some cases, it prevents the brain from overthinking. Add chamomile and lemongrass to this flowery brewed tea to boost its potency.

Chamomile has long been used as a natural sedative in Europe and can be consumed by anyone suffering from mild anxiety.

On the other hand, Chamomile provides a healthy dose of anti-inflammatory properties that help with bloating and digestive issues. Try this tea blend instead of taking a medication that might have side effects.

Flavor notes: Chamomile has a lightly sweet flavor, lemongrass has a sharp soothing flavor, and passionflower has a mild, flavorful taste. They combine to make a tasty tea that can be consumed without adding sweetener.

Ingredients:

- One tablespoon of dried passionflower (you can use fresh petals, but dried is preferable).

- One teaspoon of dried chamomile or a tablespoon of fresh ones.

- One teaspoon of dried lemongrass leaves.

- A cup of boiled water.

Instructions:

Pour the boiled water over the passionflower, chamomile, and lemongrass in a clean pot or cup. Allow to steep for 10-minutes. Strain, and add sweetener (agave, honey, or any other) if desired.

Peppermint, Ginger, and Cinnamon

Indigestion is one of many side effects of anxiety. This tea blend will help to alleviate the symptoms of indigestion. You can drink this tea whenever you eat something your body isn't used to. You'll feel more at ease, and your digestion will improve.

Imagine trying a new diet that leaves your entire body disoriented - your stomach is bloated, and you're getting restless. Its calming effect is what makes it beneficial for anxiety. Brew this tea quickly by following the simple instructions below, and you will feel better.

Flavor note: You can never have too much mint or peppermint flavor, especially on a cold morning, night, or day. The spicy taste of ginger makes this tea more soothing, and the presence of cinnamon enhances all the flavors. There will be no need for additional sweeteners if you do not like sweetened tea.

Ingredients:

- One teaspoon of cinnamon

- Two teaspoons of freshly grated ginger

- Six tablespoons of Peppermint

- Four cups of boiled water

Instructions:

In a large, preferably heatproof bowl, combine all the ingredients. Allow steeping for 15 minutes—strain and store excess in the fridge for up to three days. Serve lukewarm and sweeten to taste.

Chamomile, Ginger, Lemon, and Peppermint

This blend is similar to the lemon, ginger, and chamomile blend but with a mix of peppermint. Peppermint creates a soothing, calm herbal tea sensation that is ideal for unwinding anytime. Make a cup of this blend when you need to relax after a long day to help you feel less anxious.

Along with easing anxiety, chamomile, ginger, and peppermint tea stimulate the senses, support digestion, calm the respiratory system, and strengthen the immune system.

Flavor notes: Peppermint, ginger, and chamomile have a minty flavor, a sharp taste, and a slight sweetness that may not require additional sugar. Lemon has a mildly bitter flavor, but when combined with spicy ginger, minty Peppermint, and sweet chamomile, the bitterness is barely detectable. If you prefer a stronger bitter taste, use more lemon juice.

Ingredients:

- Two slices of Lemon.

- A teaspoon of freshly grated ginger.

- Three tablespoons of chamomile.

- Three tablespoons of fresh or 11/2 cup of dried peppermint leaves.

- Four cups of boiling water.

Instructions:

In a large pot or bowl, combine all the ingredients and pour in the boiling water—cover and steep for 15 minutes. Serve warm after straining. Keep any leftovers, but consume them within three days or discard them.

Lavender, Chamomile, Rose Petals, Calendula Petals, and Sweet Orange-Peel

Do you have trouble relaxing or falling asleep? This soothing, zero-caffeine blend can be extremely beneficial. A cup of this blend will help to relieve stress and promote more peaceful unwinding.

Because lavender promotes relaxation and relieves stress, it is an excellent addition to any herbal tea and infusions. Rose petals have effective relaxing properties, making them ideal for anxiety reduction.

On the other hand, Calendula petal has antimicrobial and antifungal properties that help tissue heal and prevent infection. Its antioxidant components aid in the fight against cancer and the prevention of heart disease and muscle fatigue. These anti-fatigue properties make it an excellent addition to this blend.

Orange peel contains pectin, which works to smooth bowel movements and prevents constipation. If your anxiety is caused by constipation or stomach upset, adding sweet orange peel to the tea will increase its effectiveness.

You can experiment with herbal tea blends to find the combination that works best for you. Many herbs have calming properties, but your body may react to some. Begin with a few spices before adding more to transform your tea into a complex blend.

This means starting with two combinations and gradually adding a third and fourth ingredient after your body responds positively to the first two. Some people prefer herbal teas with a single ingredient because they find them to be the most effective.

Flavor notes: Lavender has a minty floral flavor, while rose petals have a sweet flavor. Chamomile has a sweet taste, and when combined with sweet orange peel and calendula petals, it creates a tasty, flavorful tea blend. No sweetener is required for this tea.

Ingredients:

- One tablespoon of lavender.

- One teaspoon of orange peel.

- One tablespoon of chamomile.

- Half tablespoon of rose petals.

- One teaspoon of calendula.

- Two glasses of boiling water.

Instructions:

In a clean bowl or pot, combine all the ingredients, add the boiling water, and set aside for 15 minutes to steep. Serve immediately after straining. Any leftovers should be refrigerated and consumed within three days.

Lemon Balm and Ginger

Lemon balm is an aromatic herb that belongs to the mint family. It is primarily grown in North Africa and Europe but can now be found in any part of the world. Lemon balm's antibacterial properties make it suitable for fighting candida.

Candida is a yeast that can cause fatigue, memory problems, digestive problems, and other unusual symptoms. It also contains rosmarinic acid, which aids in activating GABA receptors in the brain, resulting in increased concentration.

Lemon balm's polyphenols, essential oils, and tannins promote mental health, strengthen the digestive system, and improve overall well-being. Its' tea, like the lemon balm used in aromatherapy, helps to relax muscles and relieves tension, muscle cramps, and headaches.

The combination of lemon balm and ginger is extremely healing. Ginger is the driving force behind this blend's anxiety-relieving properties. Although benzodiazepine drugs are used to treat anxiety, ginger's ability to reduce anxiety by affecting serotonin levels is just as effective.

Add a drop of cardamom, cinnamon, or green tea to spice up or invigorate the flavor and senses to spice up or invigorate the flavor and senses. You can tweak the blend to suit your preferences and taste buds. You can add cinnamon to any herbal tea, but you can also drink it as a standalone remedy with numerous health benefits.

Flavor notes: Lemon balm has a light, citrusy flavor. With a brush of mint, you'll feel Lemon's acidic flavor. Ginger has a more intense, sharp flavor and taste that can stimulate all your senses.

Ingredients:

- Half tablespoon of dried ginger root or two tablespoons of freshly chopped ginger root.

- One-eight cup fresh lemon balm leaves or a tablespoon of dried lemon balm.

- A cup of boiled water, honey, stevia, or other sweeteners. If you want it spicy, add more ginger!

Instructions:

Combine all the ingredients in a cup, tall glass, or Mason jar. Pour the boiling water over the mixture and set aside for 15 minutes. The longer you steep the tea, the more flavorful it becomes. Strain and reheat if necessary. Sweeten to taste.

Lavender, Lemon Balm, and Orange Tree Flower

Lavender is well-known for its calming properties; many people add it to their bath water to breathe in the softly scented aroma.

It also helps to treat insomnia by making you feel less stressed, sleepy, and relaxed.

Lemon balm has antibacterial properties, making it beneficial to the immune system.

Lemon balm's polyphenols, essential oils, and tannins promote mental health, strengthen the digestive system, and improve overall well-being.

To unwind completely after a stressful day, make this tea blend and enjoy a cup before bed.

Flavor notes: The taste of lavender is strongly minty. The lemon balm flavor is light and citrusy, and the orange tree flower flavor is all-encompassing and irresistible. The mixture may require a little sweetening.

Ingredients:
- One teaspoon of orange tree flower water.

- Three tablespoons of honey.

- Three tablespoons of lemon balm.

- Three tablespoons of lavender.

- Four cups of boiling water.

Instructions:

Take a large heatproof pot or bowl and combine all ingredients. Pour in the boiling water and steep for 15 minutes. Serve lukewarm after straining. The active ingredients work better when consumed warm rather than cold. Refrigerate any leftovers and consume them within three days. Remember to warm the tea before drinking it.

Chamomile, Ginger, and Lemon

This is the tea blend to choose if you want to start your day feeling relaxed and energized. If you had a restless night or have an interview making you nervous, make this blend and drink a cup before starting your day.

Ginger will reinvigorate you and clear your throat. The sharp flavor of ginger will wake up your taste buds as you prepare for the day. Lemon contains antioxidants that are good for your immune system and overall health. Chamomile aids relaxation, improves sleep, and reduces inflammation and menstrual pain.

A combination of these wonderful herbs will not only reduce anxiety but will also boost your immune system and provide you with a calming sensation every morning.

Flavor note: Ginger has a strong spicy flavor, and Lemon is slightly bitter. Chamomile softens all of this harshness with a healthy dose of sweetness. This one will require a sweetener.

Ingredients:

- Four slices of Lemon.

- Three tablespoons of freshly grated ginger.

- Six tablespoons of chamomile.

- Four cups of boiling water.

- Three teaspoons of honey or less (for sweetening, depending on your choice).

Instructions:

In a large heatproof bowl, combine all the ingredients, pour in the boiling water, and steep for 15 minutes. Pour into a teapot and serve. Refrigerate any leftovers for up to three days. Whenever you want some tea, warm it up as needed.

Ashwagandha, Lavender, and Rose Petals

For centuries, ashwagandha has been used to treat anxiety, insomnia, and stress. This concoction of goodness addresses the stress messages received by the nervous system. The leaves and roots of ashwagandha/winter cherry are all useful in herbal medicine.

To boost the effectiveness of the tea, combine it with lavender leaves and rose petals. All the herbs in this blend work on relaxation and reducing tension and anxiety symptoms.

Flavor notes: Ashwagandha has no taste or odor. Lavender adds a strong minty flavor to the blend, while rosemary adds a fragrant touch. You most likely will not require a sweetener.

Ingredients:

- One tablespoon of winter berries.

- One teaspoon of lavender.

- One teaspoon of rose petals.

- A cup of boiling water.

Instructions:

In a tall glass or cup, combine all the ingredients, pour in the boiling water, and set aside for 10 minutes to steep. Serve warm, with optional sweetener.

Teas are a great way to stay hydrated or when you don't want to eat large meals. In any season or climate, there is a tea that can help you feel better. For instance, a tea with ginger and mint is good for cold and flu prevention. Quickly brew them and drink them while they are still hot.

You can add lavender oil to bath water to release the active ingredient that creates a calming sensation. Lavender tea also has a calming effect. While these tea combinations' calming effects are wonderful, you can do other things to lessen anxiety.

Get daily exposure to sunlight, fresh air, and good exercise. It doesn't have to be strenuous; a quick stroll outside will do. Make an effort to eat more wholesome foods and less junk food. Steer clear of binge drinking, recreational drug use, and smoking.

Many herbal tea combinations can ease anxiety. Either buy the ingredients locally or grow them in your garden. Regardless of your preference, stick with the combination that benefits your body the most.

Please create your recipes based on the above and blend them yourself. You should speak with your doctor if you are taking any prescription drugs because some of these blends interact with them.

Chapter 10

Tea Blends for Headaches

The calming effect and comfort you get from making and drinking teas are wonderful. However, there's another reason to drink it: many types of tea have remarkable medicinal properties and are used to treat a wide range of conditions.

Headaches are one of the most common ailments known to be treated by drinking tea. It is a natural way to soothe and relax the body and, therefore, the headache.

Drinking a cup of herbal tea that blends tastiness with healing properties for headaches can help alleviate this condition that plagues people daily.

While coffee can relieve pain in some people, it can also cause or aggravate headaches in others. Caffeinated teas may have the opposite effect on your body than intended, so they are not always recommended. If you are unsure about the effects of caffeine on your headaches, stick to herbal teas. Because instead of healing, caffeinated teas will make you feel worse.

Even though headaches have been around for as long as anyone can remember, many people today treat them as minor inconveniences rather than medical emergencies. If their pain becomes intolerable, they take two pills and carry on with their day. Headaches are frequently caused by poor daily habits like dehydration, nutrient deficiency, lack of sleep, alcohol use, caffeine withdrawal, and skipping meals. All these factors contribute to headaches, and a nice hot herbal tea is the ideal remedy.

The herbs used in these teas also have nutritional benefits for the body and also taste good. Instead of being forced to take the same pill for every ache and pain, you can experiment with different tea blends to find the one that suits you best. Whether you prefer something sweet, spicy, earthy, or buttery, you'll find one you like.

This chapter will introduce you to several tea combinations that have been formulated for the express purpose of alleviating headache pain. We'll also provide step-by-step instructions for the preparation of each one.

Tea Blends and Headaches

Headaches range from mildly annoying to completely intolerable and can seriously disrupt your daily life.

You've tried eating healthier, drinking more water, and even changing your skincare routine, but nothing works; perhaps it's time to experiment with tea.

Having headaches regularly is exhausting, especially when you don't know what is causing them.

However, some headaches result from more serious issues, like internal or external injuries or an underlying health challenge. These potentially fatal conditions include blood clots or tumors, which a simple cup of tea won't help.

There are different types of headaches, the most common of which are tension headaches. There are also cluster headaches, which are very painful and tend to come in groups (hence the name), while migraines are more of a mild to moderate type of headache.

Whatever type of headache you are suffering from, a warm cup of tea may help you deal with the distracting, throbbing pain in your head. The recipes outlined in this chapter will help you find relief.

How to Identify Tea Flavor Notes

Even seasoned tea drinkers have difficulty describing the taste combinations of various tea flavors. The following are the main flavor groups that you'll notice in your tea. You're welcome to use these groups as mental checklists while you sip your tea and see if you can better discern individual tastes.

1. Floral

Floral notes can be subtle or strong; several teas contain floral notes that can bring flowers like orchids, roses, jasmine, chestnuts, and other roasted nuts to your mind.

2. Nutty

The teas with these undertones may taste like roasted chestnuts, hazelnuts, or other nuts.

3. Buttery

Certain teas feature undertones of butter. They might remind you of cream, butter, and milk.

4. Sweet

Teas that have no flavorings or sweeteners may have a pleasant natural sweetness. These teas could have vanilla, caramel, honey, or burnt sugar aromas.

5. Spices

Some teas have a savory, baking-spice-like flavor. You might detect hints of pepper, ginger, nutmeg, cinnamon, or cloves.

6. Smoky

These teas have tobacco, toast, smoky, or leather flavors.

7. Fruity

There are delicate fruity flavors in many teas. These include tropical fruits, berries, and stone fruits, including peaches and apricots.

8. Oceanic

Certain teas feature notes of the ocean, especially Japanese teas. They may have a flavor that you associate with shellfish, sea breeze, and seaweed. Some teas possess peculiar umami flavors.

9. Mineral

Teas can have mineral-like notes. They can remind you of chalk and granite, just like some types of wine.

10. Terrain

Some teas' range of earthy notes includes moss, oak, mushrooms, moist leaves, and pine.

11. Green

Some teas feature grass notes similar to sweet grass, hay, or a recently mowed lawn.

12. Plants

Peas, spinach, asparagus, and other vegetable flavors are present in some teas.

13. Phytoplankton

Several teas still taste like herbs, even if they are not herbal. These include fennel, lavender, mint, and thyme notes.

14. Body

Even though it is not a peculiar taste like the ones listed above, the body of the tea is another factor to consider. Does it have a flavor that stays on your tongue and a rich, thick body? Is it lightweight?

Different Teas and How They Taste

While each tea has its own flavor profile, most tea categories share some traits. For example, the majority of black teas taste similar to green tea. You'll find examples of the common flavors in various tea types below.

Black Tea Flavor Notes

The flavor and taste of black teas are full-bodied and robust. The following are also flavor notes for black tea:

- Earthy

- Fruity

- Malty

- Sweet

- Smoky

Green Tea Flavor Notes

Green teas are quickly steamed or pan-fired after harvest to prevent further oxidation. Green tea flavor notes might include the following:

- Grassy
- Herbaceous
- Vegetal
- Nutty
- Oceanic

White Tea Flavor Notes

Because of how they are prepared, white teas are known for their delicate and light feel. These teas have undergone minimal processing. The following are the flavor notes for white tea:

- Fruity
- Sweet
- Floral
- Buttery
- Herbaceous

Oolong Tea Flavor Notes

These teas are partially oxidized tea that shares many similarities with green and black tea. Oolong tea has the following flavor notes:

- Mineral

- Buttery

- Floral

- Fruity

- Grassy

Pu-erh Tea Flavor Notes

They are fermented partially and are well-aged. The flavor notes of Pur-erh include:

- Smooth

- Earthy

- Rich

- Smoky

- Mushroom

Matcha Tea Flavor Note

Matcha tea is a form of green tea. It is a stone-ground, shade-grown powdered tea. This tea flavor notes include:

- Umami

- Sweet

- Vegetal

- Bitter

- Smooth

Tea Blend Recipes for Headaches

You don't want to make a complicated tea blend when you have a headache. You don't have to worry about that because these recipes have you covered. Simply following the step-by-step instructions will get you on your way to relief.

Each of these tea blends has been carefully crafted to address the different types of headaches, allowing you to find the one that's right for you. Plus, with so many flavors to choose from, there's bound to be one that appeals to you. Because of the variety of herbal teas available, each has a distinct flavor profile. For example, rooibos tea has a stronger flavor and a hint of natural sweetness, while chamomile tea is floral and light.

Chamomile and Lavender Tea Blend

This headache tea recipe is easy to make and uses two ingredients found in most kitchens: chamomile and lavender. The scent from these ingredients alone is soothing and stress-relieving, making it ideal for relieving headaches. Lavender and chamomile also help with insomnia, making it an excellent choice for a cup of tea before bed.

Ingredients:

- One teaspoon (tsp) of dried chamomile or one tablespoon (Tsp) of fresh chamomile

- Half tsp of dried lavender or one and a half tsp of fresh lavender

- One cup of water

Ingredients for tea blend bags:

- One chamomile tea bag

- One lavender tea bag

- Eight ounces of hot water

Instructions for tea bag:

1. Steep the chamomile and lavender bags in hot water for five minutes

2. Remove the tea bags after five minutes and enjoy

Instructions for plain leaves:

1. Steep the leaves in hot water for 15 minutes

2. Strain the tea out into a cup or jar after the given time and enjoy

Flavor Notes: The cup of chamomile and lavender tea has a honey-like sweetness and mild apple undertones. Despite its velvety mouthfeel, this herbal tea is pure and softly flowery. The notes of this tea are earthy and floral.

Lavender Mint Tea Blend

Here's a recipe for a tea blend that helps with headache relief. Lavender has a calming and soothing effect. Mint alleviates stress and aids digestion. Lavender Mint comprises just two ingredients: calming peppermint and fragrant lavender, both known for their therapeutic properties.

Ingredients:

- Half tsp of dried lavender or one and a half tsp of fresh lavender

- Half tsp of dried mint or one and a half tsp of fresh mint

- Eight ounces of boiling water

- Honey, to taste (optional)

Instructions:

1. Combine lavender buds and mint leaves in a teapot

2. Add boiling water. Allow steeping for 5-7 minutes.

3. Sweeten with honey, if desired. Serve hot

Flavor Note: Lavender tea has a distinct flavor and aroma. Lavender tea has undertones of mint and rosemary. Some blends have a smokey or woody flavor, while others are sweeter and more floral. Lavender tea contains rose, earthy flavors, and green apples, which are similar to those found in green tea.

Peppermint, Lavender, Lemon, and Ginger Tea Blend

One popular tea combination is peppermint and lavender. Peppermint provides the alertness you require without the use of caffeinated teas. You can make this tea with either bagged or loose-leaf peppermint blends.

Ingredients:

- Half cup of dried peppermint leaves

- One-third cup of dried lavender

- Five peeled and dried lemons

- One cup of thin peeled ginger, dried

Instructions:

1. Mix peppermint with lavender, lemon, and ginger in a bowl or jar

2. Add eight ounces of hot water

3. Allow for a few minutes of steeping

4. Strain into a glass jar

5. Serve hot

Flavor Note: This tea has a refreshing mint flavor that can help relieve headaches. If you're feeling sluggish, the peppermint in the tea can help perk you up.

Ginger and Turmeric Tea Blend

This is a ginger and turmeric tea recipe. Turmeric has been shown to relieve headaches, and when combined with ginger, it creates a powerful combination.

Ingredients:

- One teaspoon of grated ginger

- One teaspoon of ground turmeric

- One cup of boiling water

- Honey (to taste)

- Lemon (optional)

Instructions:

1. Add the ginger and turmeric to a cup of boiling water

2. Let it steep for 5 minutes

3. Add honey and lemon to taste

4. Serve hot, and enjoy

Flavor Note: Turmeric and ginger are both members of the ginger family, but turmeric has a more bitter earthy note, whereas ginger has a distinct lemon-citrus flavor with earthy, warm notes.

Rosemary & Lemongrass Headache Tea Blend

When you feel a tension headache coming on, this tea blend is ideal. Rosemary relieves muscle tension, while lemongrass helps to clear your mind and improve your mood.

Ingredient:

- One teaspoon of dried rosemary

- One teaspoon of dried lemongrass

- One cup boiling water

Instructions:

1. Add the dried herbs to a cup or mug

2. Pour boiling water over the herbs and allow to steep for 5 minutes

3. Strain the tea and enjoy

Flavor Notes: The rosemary and lemongrass flavors are the most prominent in this tea blend. It also has a hint of bitterness from the rosemary being the herbaceous flavor and lemongrass having a sweet, strong lemony taste. If the bitterness is too strong for you, add a little honey to taste.

Cinnamon & Licorice Tea Blend

This tea blend is an excellent way to relieve stress and headaches. The licorice root will help to relax the body, and the cinnamon will help to relieve tension headache.

Ingredients:
- One teaspoon of licorice root
- One teaspoon of cinnamon
- One cup of water

Instructions:
1. Add the licorice root and cinnamon to a cup of boiling water

2. Let the tea steep for 10 minutes

3. Strain the tea and drink it slowly

Flavor Note: Cinnamon has a spicy, slightly woody flavor note, and licorice has a woody flavor similar to cinnamon. It's sweet, somewhat floral, and woody, with a mild bitterness beneath the main flavor.

Passionflower and Lemon Balm Tea Blend

This tea blend is ideal if you are feeling tense and need to unwind. The passion flower will calm your nerves, while the lemon balm will calm your mind.

Ingredients:

- One teaspoon of dried passion flower

- One teaspoon of dried lemon balm

- One cup of boiling water

Instructions:

1. Mix all the dry herbs together in a bowl

2. Add a cup of boiling water

3. Allow for a 5–10-minute steep

4. Sweeten with honey (Optional)

5. Serve hot, and enjoy

Flavor Note: The flavors of passion flower and lemon balm are potent. The lemon balm gives the passion flower a floral and citrusy flavor.

Turmeric and Cinnamon Tea Blend

This recipe is a great choice if you're looking for an antioxidant tea with anti-inflammatory properties.

Ingredients:

- One teaspoon of turmeric

- One teaspoon of ground cinnamon

- One cup boiling water

- One tablespoon of honey (optional)

- One tablespoon of milk (optional)

Instructions:

1. Combine the turmeric, cinnamon, and boiling water in a mug

2. Let it steep for 5 minutes

3. Strain the tea and add honey and milk if desired

4. Serve hot, and enjoy!

Flavor Notes: Turmeric has an earthy bitter taste, whereas cinnamon has a mildly sweet and spicy taste.

Tulsi, Licorice Root, and Clove Tea Blend

This is a recipe for tulsi, licorice root, and clove tea. This mixture is said to help relieve tension headaches.

Ingredients:

- Half cup of tulsi

- Half cup of licorice root

- One-quarter tablespoon of cloves

- Eight ounces of water

Instructions:

1. Start by boiling water and then adding tulsi leaves, licorice root, and cloves

2. Allow the mixture to steep for 10 minutes

3. Strain the mixture and sweeten with honey if desired

4. Serve hot. Enjoy!

Flavor Note: This tea blend's most prominent flavor notes are spice from the cloves, sweetness from the licorice root, and a floral note from the tulsi leaves.

Coriander Tea Blend

This tea contains coriander, ginger, and turmeric. Coriander tastes citrusy, whereas ginger tastes spicy and earthy. Turmeric lends a slightly bitter flavor to this blend.

Ingredients:

- One teaspoon of coriander seeds

- One teaspoon of grated ginger

- One-fourth teaspoon of ground turmeric

- One cup of water

- Honey, to taste

Instructions:

1. Toast the coriander seeds in a pan over medium heat for a few minutes until they become fragrant.

2. Add the ginger and turmeric, and toast for another minute.

3. Add the water and bring it to a boil.

4. Remove from the heat and leave to steep for 5 minutes.

5. Strain and sweeten with honey to taste.

Flavor Note: Coriander has an earthy, warm flavor that is not spicy. It has a citrus undertone and a mild floral flavor.

Willow Bark Tea Blend

Willow bark is an excellent remedy for headaches because it contains salicin, a natural pain reliever.

Ingredients:

- One teaspoon of willow bark

- One cup of water

- Honey (optional)

Instructions:

1. Add a cup of boiling water to the willow bark

2. Allow for ten (10) minutes of steeping

3. Add honey to taste

4. Serve hot!

The most prominent flavor notes in willow bark tea are bitter and astringent. If you find the taste too intense, add lemon juice or mint leaves to help round out the flavor.

Butterbur Tea Blend

This tea blend has long been used to treat headaches and migraines. Some studies have found that it can help reduce the frequency of migraines.

Ingredients:

- One teaspoon of dried butterbur

- Eight ounces of boiling water

- One tablespoon of honey (optional)

- One lemon wedge (optional)

Instructions:

1. Add the butterbur to a teapot or cup

2. Pour the boiling water over it

3. Allow it to steep for 10 minutes

4. Strain the tea and add honey and lemon to taste, if desired

Flavor Note: Butterbur is light, honey-sweet, and floral, like spring.

Rosemary & Ginger Tea Blend

This is an excellent blend for those who suffer from tension headaches. Because rosemary is a muscle relaxant, it can help relieve the tension causing your headache. In addition, ginger is a well-known remedy for nausea, which is frequently a symptom of tension headaches.

Ingredients:
- One teaspoon of dried rosemary
- One teaspoon of dried ginger
- One cup boiling water

Instructions:
1. Steep the herbs in boiling water for 5-10 minutes
2. Strain out the tea into a jar or cup
3. Serve hot with either lemon or honey if it tastes too strong

Flavor Note: Rosemary has an herbaceous flavor, whereas ginger has a warm earthy aroma with underlying citrus-lemon notes.

Your first step should be to see your doctor about your headache symptoms and possible treatments (prescription and over-the-counter). It might take a while to discover a treatment that works for your headaches if they're severe. You can also try alternative therapies, like using a hot or cold pack, turning down the lights, resting, meditating, or sipping some herbal tea.

Teas, including butterbur, citron, and curcumin, are more beneficial in controlling and relieving headache symptoms than placebos, compounds with no therapeutic benefits. Consult your doctor about experimenting with various tea recipes to supplement your medications and relieve headaches.

In conclusion, there is no one-size-fits-all solution for headaches. However, numerous tea blends can help alleviate the discomfort. Combining different ingredients can make a tea tailored to your specific needs.

Tea is a versatile beverage that can be consumed hot or cold and is available in various flavors. So, if you're looking for a new way to relieve headaches, why not try tea? You're sure to find the perfect tea blend for you with so many different recipes to choose from.

Conclusion

Tea gardening is a great way to enjoy the flavor of freshly grown tea. You can grow, plant, harvest, create, and prepare your own tea, which is often better than store-bought types. What initially appears to be a daunting task is always a soothing and relaxing activity.

Growing your tea garden will give you a diverse selection of tea blends. Your creative energy is released, and you produce delectable recipes for every day, season, and weather condition.

When planning your garden, keep in mind the growth conditions discussed in earlier chapters. Tea plants and herbs need the right site, temperature, water content, etc., to thrive. You should also devote sufficient time to compiling a comprehensive plant index.

Grow the most important and useful plants, whose flowers, leaves, stems, and fruits can all be consumed. Follow the step-by-step instructions for growing herbs and tea plants in your garden.

Once your plants are ready for harvest, follow all protocols to get the most out of your tea plants. There is an ideal way to harvest your plants for tea, from the flowers to the root. Follow the instructions in this book, and you'll be set.

Keep a watch out for all potential diseases that could affect your tea plant and take all preventative measures to avoid infection on your plants; in the case of an existing infection, ensure that you have taken note of all treatment methods.

As a beginner, this book guides you through each process, from tilling the soil to sipping a cup of hot tea. You'll learn about tea gardening, its uses, the equipment needed, the different types of tea, and its history. All the information you need to become a successful tea garden owner has been laid out, so you no longer need to worry about making a mistake or missing an opportunity.

This book explains in depth the significance of growing your tea. Herbal tea gives your body the necessary nutrients, minerals, vitamins, and antioxidants. It is also effective as a treatment for various ailments, including inflammation, arthritis, etc. Tea helps with digestion, relieves stress, reduces nasal congestion, encourages breathing, and treats irritable bowel syndrome.

Aside from the many physical benefits, a hot cup of tea can work like magic on anxiety. In a state of distress, apprehension, and pressure, tea's soothing properties offer peace of mind and total calmness.

That's all you need to get started with your own tea garden! Remember to be patient and enjoy the process; after all, the journey, not the destination, is what matters. Get your shovel, hoe, garden fork, and other gardening implements out of storage and get to work.

Thank you for buying and reading/listening to our book. If you found this book useful/helpful, please take a few minutes and leave a review on Amazon.com or Audible.com (if you bought the audio version).

References

History of Tea - Learn About Tea History. (n.d.).
Coffeeteawarehouse.Com.
http://www.coffeeteawarehouse.com/tea-history.html

UK Tea & Infusions Association - History of Tea. (n.d.).
Tea.Co.Uk. https://www.tea.co.uk/history-of-tea

Farrell, A. (2020, October 22). How to Create Your Own Herbal
Tea Garden. The New York Times.
https://www.nytimes.com/2020/10/22/t-magazine/how-to-
grow-herbal-tea-garden.html

floristkid team. (2022, February 1). How To Build An Herbal Tea
Garden At Home. Florist Kid | Kids Gardening | School
Garden | Microgreens. https://floristkid.com/herbal-tea-
garden/

Gardening Tools We Consider Indispensable: It Doesn't Take
Much! (n.d.). Almanac.Com.
https://www.almanac.com/gardening-tools-guide

Types of Tea. (n.d.). Stash Tea.
https://www.stashtea.com/blogs/education/tea-types

Elle. (2022, August 23). Guide how to grow your own tea [homegrown tea, anyone?]. Outdoor Happens. https://www.outdoorhappens.com/tea-plants-for-sale-grow-camellia-plants-and-enjoy-homegrown-tea/

Soil : Tea World - an initiative of KKHSOU. (n.d.). Kkhsou. In. http://teaworld.kkhsou.in/page-details.php?name=Soil&page=913323150eb87fb111b220ff7

Tea plants---where they grow. (n.d.). Tealeafjournal.com. http://www.tealeafjournal.com/tea-plant-2.html

Tealet. (n.d.). Tealet. https://tealet.com/usteaplanting

Foster, J. (2021, January 1). 14 factors to choose your vegetable garden location. Growit Buildit. https://growitbuildit.com/14-factors-to-choose-your-vegetable-garden-location/

Grant, A. (2017, May 23). Container-grown tea: Tips on growing tea plants in pots. Gardening Know-How. https://www.gardeningknowhow.com/edible/herbs/tea-plant/container-grown-tea-plant.htm

John, S. R.-S. (2014, March 24). How to grow your own tea container garden. Bonnie Plants. https://bonnieplants.com/blogs/garden-plans/tea-garden-containers

Grow Your Own Herbal Teas. (2016, May 17). Eartheasy Guides & Articles. https://learn.eartheasy.com/articles/grow-your-own-herbal-teas/

Chocolate Mint Care. (2021, July 13). Balcony Garden Web. https://balconygardenweb.com/chocolate-mint-care-growing-mint-in-pots/

Growing Rosemary In Pots. (2019, June 7). Balcony Garden Web. https://balconygardenweb.com/growing-rosemary-in-pots-rosemary-plant-care/

Chandrima. (2021, May 21). Growing Raspberry in Pots. Balcony Garden Web. https://balconygardenweb.com/growing-raspberry-in-pots-container-care/

Planting Strawberry. (2019, January 3). Balcony Garden Web. https://balconygardenweb.com/planting-growing-strawberries-care/

Growing Tea Leaves at Home. (2020, June 25). Balcony Garden Web. https://balconygardenweb.com/growing-tea-leaves-at-home-how-to-grow-green/

Chandrima. (2022, May 30). Small Rose Garden. Balcony Garden Web. https://balconygardenweb.com/small-rose-garden-growing-roses-in-containers-balcony-patio-and-terrace/

Bhupendra. (2022, November 1). How to Grow Lavender Plants in Home and Garden. Balcony Garden Web. https://balconygardenweb.com/how-to-grow-lavender-plants-growing-lavender/

Harlow, I. (2015, March 13). How to grow, harvest and preserve herbs for tea. Farm and Dairy. https://www.farmanddairy.com/top-stories/grow-tea-garden/245189.html

How to grow, care for, and harvest your own tea garden. (2017, August 20). Gardening Channel. https://www.gardeningchannel.com/how-to-grow-tea-garden/

Tea Plantation Guide. (n.d.). Indiaagronet.com. https://indiaagronet.com/indiaagronet/horticulture/CONTENTS/tea.htm

The Tea harvest / Dethlefsen & Balk - Tea, Coffee, Confiserie, accessories. (n.d.). Dethlefsen-balk.de. https://www.dethlefsen-balk.de/ENU/10733/The_Tea_Harvest.html

Gowda, M. p. n. (n.d.). Diseases of tea. Slideshare.net. https://www.slideshare.net/maheshpngowda1/diseases-of-tea

Life & Agri. (2020, October 23). Pest and diseases in a Tea Plantation - What is a Tea plantation? Lifeandagri.com; Life and Agri. https://lifeandagri.com/pest-and-diseases-in-a-tea-plantation/

Tea. (n.d.). Psu.edu. https://plantvillage.psu.edu/topics/tea/infos

Tea Diseases. (n.d.). Vikaspedia.In. https://vikaspedia.in/agriculture/crop-production/integrated-pest-managment/ipm-for-commercial-crops/ipm-strategies-for-tea/tea-diseases

Zhao, X., Chen, S., Wang, S., Shan, W., Wang, X., Lin, Y., Su, F., Yang, Z., & Yu, X. (2019). Defensive responses of tea plants (Camellia sinensis) against tea green Leafhopper attack: A multi-omics study. Frontiers in Plant Science, 10, 1705. https://doi.org/10.3389/fpls.2019.01705

AdCeler. (2021, October 27). A pure, single ingredient tea has its charm and can be a pure, pleasing experience for the palate. However. Solaris Tea. https://solarisbotanicals.com/blogs/lifestyle/what-is-a-tea-blend

(amp), A. (2021, May 28). The benefits of tea blending. Bloem & Moi. https://www.bloemetmoi.com/benefits-of-tea-blending/

Correspondent, H. T. (2018, December 29). The art of tea blending - how to blend flavours for your perfect cup of tea. The Hindustan Times. https://www.hindustantimes.com/more-lifestyle/the-art-of-tea-blending-how-to-blend-flavours-for-your-perfect-cup-of-tea/story-EoWNkvulAKGFCLKzLMSioJ.html

Fusion Teas. (2020, September 3). Which tea flavors blend best together. Fusion Teas Blog. https://blog.fusionteas.com/which-tea-flavors-blend-best-together/

Manchanda, S. (2019, January 17). The art of tea blending. Tea Trunk. https://teatrunk.in/blogs/editorial/the-art-of-tea-blending

Pannunzio, L. A. (2021, June 15). The art of tea blending - 6 tips for creating your own tea blends. The Cup of Life; Lu Ann Pannunzio. https://theteacupoflife.com/2021/06/the-art-of-tea-blending-creating-your-own-tea-blends.html

Scarborough, S. (2020, December 23). The art of blending tea. Firepot.com. https://blog.firepot.com/journal/the-art-of-blending-tea

Sharma, M. (2015, July 23). 8 tips for creating your own tea blends. Tea Stories - Still Steeping: Teabox Blog. https://blog.teabox.com/diy-tea-blends

Shea, T. (2020, December 9). Four incredibly harmful effects artificial dyes have on our health. Foodnerd. https://www.foodnerdinc.com/blogs/food-for-thought/artificial-food-coloring-no-thank-you

Stein, S. (n.d.). 8 tea blends with awesome health benefits. Canadian Living. https://www.canadianliving.com/health/nutrition/article/8-tea-blends-with-awesome-health-benefits

Tea blending guide: How to make tea blends. (2021, August 26). Hummingbird Tea Room. https://hummingbirdtearoom.com/tea-blending-guide-how-to-make-tea-blends/

Tea hub. (n.d.). Jenierteas.com. https://jenierteas.com/tea-hub/?p=quick-guide-to-tea-blending-ingredients-for-your-tea-blends

Tea, S. (2021, July 13). Tea blending 101. Shanti Tea. https://www.shantitea.ca/home/blog_article/st/151795/tea-blending-101

Tips for blending. (n.d.). I Blend My Tea. https://www.iblendmytea.com/pages/tips-for-blending

What are tea blends? How do they compare to pure teas? (n.d.). Matcha Alternatives. https://matchaalternatives.com/blogs/the-ma-blog/what-are-tea-blends

What is blend tea and the benefits of tea blending. (n.d.).
Runmingtea.com. https://www.runmingtea.com/What-Is-
Blend-Tea-And-The-Benefits-Of-Tea-Blending-n-52/

(N.d.-a). Bellaallnatural.com.
https://www.bellaallnatural.com/blogs/learn/mixing-blend-
tea-flavors

(N.d.-b). Teafloor.com. https://teafloor.com/blog/the-art-of-tea-
blending/

7 tips to brew better tasting tea. (n.d.). Red Blossom Tea Company.
https://redblossomtea.com/blogs/red-blossom-blog/7-tips-
to-brew-better-tasting-tea

Bawden-Davis, J. (n.d.). How to grow, harvest and brew homemade
herb tea. Gardentech.com.
https://www.gardentech.com/blog/gardening-and-healthy-
living/growing-and-brewing-your-own-tea

Bilow, R. (2015, September 30). Steep your way to hot tea
perfection by avoiding these common mistakes. Bon
Appétit. https://www.bonappetit.com/test-kitchen/common-
mistakes/article/hot-tea-common-mistakes

Choe, J. (2018, September 19). How to easily make a proper cup of
tea. Oh, How Civilized.
https://www.ohhowcivilized.com/how-to-correctly-brew-a-
cup-of-tea/

Choe, J. (2020, May 1). Cold brew tea: What it is & how to make it
properly. Oh, How Civilized.
https://www.ohhowcivilized.com/make-best-iced-tea-cold-
brew/

frenchpresscoffee. (2015, December 18). How to Make Perfect Tea
     With a French Press. Instructables.
     https://www.instructables.com/How-to-Make-Perfect-Tea-
     With-a-French-Press/

Gaiwan tea preparation. (n.d.). The Fragrant Leaf.
     https://thefragrantleaf.com/pages/gaiwan-tea-preparation

Goodwin, L. (2009, December 29). The right water temperature for
     brewing any type of tea. The Spruce Eats.
     https://www.thespruceeats.com/how-to-brew-tea-water-
     temperatures-766316

Heidi. (n.d.). Guide to brewing tea. Mountainroseherbs.com.
     https://blog.mountainroseherbs.com/guide-to-tea-brewing

How to brew the perfect cup of tea. (n.d.). Twinings North
     America. https://twiningsusa.com/pages/how-to-brew-the-
     perfect-cup-of-tea

How to steep hot tea. (2010, March 31). The Republic of Tea.
     https://the.republicoftea.com/tea-library/tea-101/how-to-
     brew-hot-tea/

Kate. (2015, June 28). Cold brew iced tea. Cookie and Kate.
     https://cookieandkate.com/cold-brew-iced-tea/

Macropoulos, K. (2011, June 28). What is the difference between
     brewing tea & steeping tea? Livestrong.com.
     https://www.livestrong.com/article/480185-what-is-the-
     difference-between-brewing-tea-steeping-tea/

Nast, C. (2017, June 9). How to brew tea perfectly every time.
     Epicurious. https://www.epicurious.com/expert-advice/how-
     to-brew-tea-perfectly-article

Simple Loose Leaf. (2021, March 10). How to make tea on the stove. Simple Loose Leaf Tea Company. https://simplelooseleaf.com/blog/brewing-tea/how-to-make-tea-stove/

Tea, G. M. (n.d.). How to make hot brewed iced tea. Golden Moon Tea. https://www.goldenmoontea.com/blogs/tea/106694279-how-to-make-hot-brewed-iced-tea

The benefits of drinking hot tea. (2022, March 3). K Brew | K Brew. https://www.knoxvillebrew.com/03/the-benefits-of-drinking-hot-tea/

What is Chai? (2016, February 12). The Republic of Tea. https://the.republicoftea.com/tea-library/black-tea/what-is-chai/

(N.d.). Sipsby.com. https://www.sipsby.com/blogs/tea-recipes/cold-brew-tea#announcement--1

Camila. (2022, December 9). The best 14 herbal teas for calming stress and anxiety. Brewed Leaf Love. https://brewedleaflove.com/herbal-tea-stress-anxiety/

5 herbal tea recipes to relieve anxiety and stress. (2021, March 2). Bettersleep.com. https://www.bettersleep.com/blog/5-herbal-tea-recipe-to-relieve-anxiety-and-stress/

Meghan. (2022, April 21). Top 10 best teas for anxiety to stay calm & stress free! Afternoonteareads.com. https://afternoonteareads.com/top-10-best-teas-for-anxiety-to-stay-calm/

the Healthline Medical Network, & Coelho, S. (2022, June 23). The 20 best teas for anxiety in 2022. Healthline; Healthline Media. https://www.healthline.com/health/anxiety/tea-for-anxiety

Godbole, N. (2020, April 18). Calm your anxiety with these herbal teas. Thrillist. https://www.thrillist.com/drink/nation/best-herbal-tea-for-anxiety

Wack, M. (2021, September 1). Calming tea: The 5 best teas for anxiety and stress. ArtfulTea. https://artfultea.com/blogs/wellness/teas-for-stress

Osborn, C. O. (2018, June 19). Headache tea: Best herbal teas for headaches and where to find T. Healthline. https://www.healthline.com/health/headache-tea

Types and grades of tea. (n.d.). Frontiercoop.com. https://www.frontiercoop.com/community/guides/types-and-grades-tea

What does tea taste like? A guide to tea tasting notes. (2022, January 14). ArtfulTea. https://artfultea.com/blogs/tea-wisdom/what-does-tea-taste-like-a-guide-to-tea-tasting-notes

(N.d.). Myteadrop.com. https://www.myteadrop.com/blogs/news/the-7-best-teas-for-headaches

Jagdish. (2015, April 6). Tea Farming information detailed guide. Agri Farming. https://www.agrifarming.in/tea-farming-information

Farrell, A. (2020, October 22). How to Create Your Own Herbal Tea Garden. The New York Times. https://www.nytimes.com/2020/10/22/t-magazine/how-to-grow-herbal-tea-garden.html

How to grow tea. (n.d.). Love The Garden. https://www.lovethegarden.com/uk-en/article/how-grow-tea